ENDORSEMENTS

"Who among us has not had heart and mind stirred by a Watts hymn? Here we learn the story behind the hymns. We learn of a Christ-centered life, a doxological life. And from that wellspring has come the hymns we love to sing. Watts's hymns are a gift for the church, and so is this biography by Douglas Bond."

—DR. STEPHEN J. NICHOLS
President, Reformation Bible College
Sanford, Florida

"We all know and love 'Joy to the World,' 'Jesus Shall Reign,' 'Alas and Did My Savior Bleed,' 'When I Survey the Wondrous Cross,' 'O God, Our Help in Ages Past,' and a host of his other compositions. And yet, most Christians know precious little about the author of these great hymn texts—the man history has dubbed as the 'Father of English Hymnody.' At least, until now. Thanks to the prolific and eloquent pen of Douglas Bond, we now have an insightful glimpse into the life, the faith, and the poetic wonder of this remarkable servant of the church: Isaac Watts. This delightful book needs to be put at the top of your must-read list."

—DR. GEORGE GRANT
Pastor, Parish Presbyterian Church
Franklin, Tennessee

The Poetic Wonder *of*

Isaac Watts

The Long Line of Godly Men Profiles

Series editor, Steven J. Lawson

The Expository Genius of John Calvin
by Steven J. Lawson
The Unwavering Resolve of Jonathan Edwards
by Steven J. Lawson
The Mighty Weakness of John Knox
by Douglas Bond
The Gospel Focus of Charles Spurgeon
by Steven J. Lawson
The Heroic Boldness of Martin Luther
by Steven J. Lawson
The Poetic Wonder of Isaac Watts
by Douglas Bond
The Evangelistic Zeal of George Whitefield
by Steven J. Lawson
The Trinitarian Devotion of John Owen
by Sinclair B. Ferguson
The Daring Mission of William Tyndale
by Steven J. Lawson
The Passionate Preaching of Martyn Lloyd-Jones
by Steven J. Lawson

A **Long Line of Godly Men** Profile

The Poetic Wonder *of*

Isaac Watts

DOUGLAS BOND

Reformation Trust A DIVISION OF LIGONIER MINISTRIES, ORLANDO, FL

The Poetic Wonder of Isaac Watts

© 2013 by Douglas Bond
Published by Reformation Trust Publishing
a division of Ligonier Ministries
421 Ligonier Court, Sanford, FL 32771
Ligonier.org   ReformationTrust.com

Printed in Crawfordsville, Indiana
LSC Communications
September 2016
First edition, second printing

Cover design: Chris Larson
Cover illustration: Kent Barton
Interior design and typeset: Katherine Lloyd, The DESK

Library of Congress Cataloging-in-Publication Data

Bond, Douglas, 1958-
The poetic wonder of Isaac Watts / Douglas Bond.
pages cm -- (The long line of godly men profile)
Includes bibliographical references and index.

ISBN 978-1-56769-308-9

1. Watts, Isaac, 1674-1748--Criticism and interpretation. 2. Christian poetry,
English--18th century--History and criticism. 3. Christianity and literature-
-England--History--18th century. I. Title.

PR3763.W2Z59 2013
821'.5--dc23

2013028528

To my wife

TABLE OF CONTENTS

Foreword   Followers Worthy to Be Followed xi

Preface   Doxology for All Time x

Chapter One   Watts' Life and Legacy 1

Chapter Two   Watts as Educator. 27

Chapter Three Watts' Sermon Hymns 37

Chapter Four Watts as Lyric Poet 49

Chapter Five Watts as Hymn Writer. 57

Chapter Six   Watts as Poet Theologian. 71

Chapter Seven Watts as Children's Poet 85

Chapter Eight Watts as Psalm Interpreter. 99

Conclusion   Watts for Our Time 121

Appendix A: An Isaac Watts Timeline. 139

Appendix B: Favorite Isaac Watts Hymns 143

Appendix C: Books by Isaac Watts 145

Notes. 149

Bibliography 157

Index. 161

Followers Worthy to Be Followed

Down through the centuries, God has providentially raised up a long line of godly men, whom He has mightily used at strategic moments in church history. These valiant soldiers of the cross have come from all walks of life—from the ivy-covered halls of elite schools to the dusty back rooms of tradesmen's shops. They have arisen from all points of this world—from highly visible venues in densely populated cities to obscure hamlets in remote places. Yet despite these differences, these pivotal figures have had much in common.

Each man possessed an unwavering faith in the Lord Jesus Christ. But more can be said about these luminous figures. Each of these stalwarts of the faith held deep convictions in the God-exalting truths known as the doctrines of grace. Though they differed in secondary matters of theology, they stood shoulder to shoulder in championing these five biblical teachings that magnify the sovereign grace of God in salvation. They upheld the foundational truth that "salvation is of the Lord" (Ps. 3:8; Jonah 2:9).

Far from paralyzing these spiritual giants, the doctrines of grace enflamed their hearts with reverential awe for God and humbled their souls before His throne. The truths of sovereign grace emboldened these men to rise up and advance the cause of Christ on the earth. Any survey of history reveals that those who embrace these Reformed truths are granted extraordinary confidence in their God. With an enlarged vision of His saving grace, they stepped forward boldly and accomplished the work of ten, even twenty men. They arose with wings like eagles and soared over their times in human history. Experientially, the doctrines of grace empowered them to serve God in their divinely appointed hour, leaving a godly influence upon future generations.

This *Long Line of Godly Men Profile* series highlights key figures in the age-long procession of sovereign-grace men. The purpose of this series is to explore how these figures used their God-given gifts and abilities to impact their times and further the kingdom of heaven. Because they were courageous followers of Christ, their examples are worthy of emulation today.

The focus of this next volume is upon the preeminent English hymn writer Isaac Watts. The poetic beauty of his doctrinally steeped hymns transcend the centuries and continue to enrich the church today. By his extraordinary literary skill, he made hymn-singing a devotional force in the Protestant church. Captured by a towering vision of God, this gifted composer revitalized congregational singing by restating rich theology in lyrics that matched the musical style with the weightiness of the biblical message. All this—the rise and fall of a phrase, striking metaphors, the cadence of the line—conveyed the majesty and transcendence of God in unforgettable words. Called the Melanchthon of his times, this pastor-hymnologist influenced the course of congregational worship that has lasted until this day. His hymns remain a staple in the spiritual life of the church.

This gift for poetic wonder is needed, once again, in this present hour. In a day where there is much shallowness in corporate worship, the church must recapture a high view of God that leads to transcendent worship. In the final analysis, it is theology that inevitably produces doxology. The recent resurgence of Reformed theology must inspire towering praise in the hearts of believers. May the Lord use this book to ignite a new generation to "survey the wondrous cross on which the Prince of glory died."

Soli Deo gloria!

— *Steven J. Lawson*

Series editor

Doxology
for All Time

It was an autumn Sunday evening in 1976 when, as a seventeen-year-old, the gospel of grace alone through faith alone in Christ alone became irrevocably real to my soul. I remember it vividly: the awakened hearing of truths I had been tenderly taught since my earliest recollections, the sense of wonder at divine grace, and the experiential thrill of the reality of the cross and of Christ my Savior shedding His blood, suffering and dying in my place, for my sin and my guilt. I remember hot tears stinging my cheeks as the genuineness of grace and the gospel washed over me that evening.

With a trembling hand and a heart nearly bursting with love and gratitude for the free grace of God, I reached for the elements of bread and wine, Christ therein pictured, symbolized, and made spiritually real before me.

What was the means that awakened a young man that glorious evening? Was it an entertaining sermon delivered by a celebrity preacher? Was it the emotional hype concocted by the latest Christian rock band? Was it high-church ceremony attempting to fabricate the transcendent? No, it was none of these.

It was Isaac Watts.

I had sung the words of his hymn at Communion every month for eleven years, but that evening, Watts' rich poetry dazzled my imagination and made a deep and lasting impression on my heart. It's not cool at seventeen to weep publicly, but I wept, and though I did, I managed to join Watts in his slack-jawed wonder at the cross.

When I survey the wondrous cross
On which the Prince of glory died,
My richest gain I count but loss,
And pour contempt on all my pride.[1]

By his incomparable imagination, Watts transported me back to hot, dusty Golgotha, where I heard the thudding of the hammer on the spikes, the taunting and spitting, the moaning and wails of sorrow. With Watts' words, I became the young man surveying that wondrous cross. With eyes of faith, I was the one seeing the Prince of glory forsaken by His Father and dying in anguish. And because I was now seeing it, I was the one resolving to count but loss all my aspirations to riches and greatness. I was, for the first time, pouring contempt on all my delusional pride of body and mind.

> *Forbid it, Lord, that I should boast,*
> *Save in the cross of Christ my God:*
> *All the vain things that charm me most,*
> *I sacrifice them to his blood.*

Watts, by his sense of wonder at the cross of Christ, and with skillful strokes of his poetic pen, showed me the absurdity of my view of the world. He deftly stirred up in me the ugliness and utter inappropriateness of my pride and boasting, my preoccupation with empty things that so captivated my teen world. By vividly holding before me the cross of Jesus, he demanded that I drop everything and reckon with it. By his words, Watts compelled me to join him, to see with him the One who hung on that cross for me.

> *See from his head, his hands, his feet,*
> *Sorrow and love flow mingled down:*
> *Did e'er such love and sorrow meet,*
> *Or thorns compose so rich a crown?*

Watts' rhetorical question caused me to see how ridiculous my sense of value had been. I had been scrambling after the world's riches, wisdom, and entertainments. But Watts held before me Christ—His head, His hands, His feet—and the surpassing richness of His thorny crown. It was as if I was there and could see it, hear Him groaning, and feel the penetration of each thorn in His brow. I was compelled to respond.

Were the whole realm of nature mine,
That were a present far too small;
Love so amazing, so divine,
Demands my soul, my life, my all.

Watts assaulted my deeply flawed value system with this closing quatrain. How absurd it was for me to think that I could own every piece of wealth in the entire natural world, and then to imagine that I could offer it as a gift, and it would somehow be proportionate to Jesus Himself. With a few strokes of his quill, Watts smashed all that for me. His imaginative comparison of all the temporal riches of nature heaped up as a present on one side, and the atoning sacrifice of Jesus Christ for my sins on the other, shamed me; it made me "hide my blushing face while His dear cross appeared."[2]

In sixteen short lines of poetry, in 128 syllables, Watts demolished my twisted sense of value and drove me to my knees at the foot of that cross. He had peeled back the glitter of the temporal world, had parted the clouds with his pen, and in that parting he had dazzled me with divine love, love so amazing that it demanded my soul, my life, my all—every part of me belonged to Jesus. He purchased my life on that cross, and such amazing love for me graciously drew me, irresistibly compelled me, to want more than anything to forsake all else and follow Jesus.

WHY ISAAC WATTS?

As a consequence of having my spiritual imagination baptized by Watts' imagination, he has long held an important place in my mind and heart. When my devotion is cold and stale in public or in private, I turn to Watts, who "give[s] me the wings of faith"[3] and turns me to Jesus. I'm inclined to think that if Watts, more than two hundred years after his death, can be the means of awakening the soul of a seventeen-year-old young man, there just may be a great deal in his body of work that no generation of Christians can afford to live without.

First, we need Watts' poetry in our lives. Our world clambers after the latest thing, and as we wear ourselves out in the process, great poets such as Watts often get put in a box on the curb for the thrift store pickup. How could a gawky, male poet, living and writing three hundred years ago, be relevant today? Our postmodern, post-Christian, post-biblical culture has almost totally dismissed what was called poetry in Watts' day. Few deny it: ours is a post-poetry culture.

Martin Luther insisted that in a reformation, "We need poets."[4] However, Christians often accept the decline of poetry without a whimper. Won't the machinations of society carry on just fine without poetry? Won't the church do just fine without it? It's not like poetry contributes anything vital. You can't eat it. So thought Hanoverian King George II: "I hate all poets!" he declared. But are Christians to stand deferentially aside as culture pitches poetry—the highest form—into the lowest circle of hell?

What happened to real poetry, and why do we so desperately need Watts to help us recover it? Arguably the decline was fueled by Walt Whitman, a man with new ideas that demanded a new form. "Through me," he wrote, "forbidden voices, voices of sexes and lust, voices veiled, and I removed the veil."[5]

Whitman-like *vers libre* poetry dictates against any conventional structure of meter or rhyme, lyric elements necessary to make poetry singable, as Watts understood so well. Whitman's throw-off-the-shackles impulse created a blurring of literary genre wherein poetic form was abandoned in favor of irregular bursts of feeling. What often remains is fragmented prose. "Poetry" thus conceived provides a pseudo-form for saying private things about one's self, things one would never utter in direct speech—until Whitman removed the veil.

Such redefining of poetry has led to a proliferation of words and phrases that seem more like emotive exhibitionism penned by therapeutic zealots than anything resembling real poetry. I once heard John Stott quip about Americans, "The trouble with you Americans is you're constantly engaged in a spiritual strip-tease."[6]

Abandoning form for raw emotion is not unique to poets. Most artists are quite pleased with themselves for smashing outmoded forms in favor of new structures, ones better suited to self-expression, the now-primary sphere of art.

It's no coincidence that poetry began its descent into "gaseous emotionalizing" in egalitarian America. Alexis de Tocqueville placed the blame squarely on the devolutions of democracy: "Nothing is more repugnant to the human mind, in an age of equality, than the idea of subjection to forms." As he continued, one wonders whether de Tocqueville was thinking of Whitman: "Democracy diverts the imagination from all that is external to man, and fixes it on man alone. Each citizen is habitually engaged in the contemplation of a very puny object, namely, himself."[7]

Meanwhile, Whitman was working on his signature poem, *Song of Myself*, the prototype of vacuous praise—of the wrong object. Man-centered praise poetry was born. How vastly different from Watts, who wrote of his poetic purpose:

> *Begin, my tongue, some heav'nly theme,*
> *And speak some boundless thing.*
> *The mighty works, or mightier Name*
> *Of our eternal King.*[8]

While Watts had made Christ the theme of his poetry, Whitman's *Song of Myself* set the mortar of poetic self-referentialism. Much of his poetry is disgusting material: "I believe in the flesh and the appetites," he crooned in *Song of Myself.* "Divine am I inside and out. . . . The scent of these armpits aroma finer than prayer, [t]his head more than churches, bibles, and all the creeds. . . . Nothing, not God, is greater . . . more wonderful than myself."[9] One wishes Whitman would have stopped, but he did not. Nor have poets since.

One tragic result of Whitman and his imitators is that we have forfeited the ability to measure the quality of poetry, so free verse proliferates without censure as everyone and his cocker spaniel gets in touch with the poet within, including well-intentioned youthful worship leaders. There's little place for Watts in such a literary world. Ours is without a rudder, where poetry has no boundaries, no canvas, no walls, no arches, no vaulted ceilings—and, hence, no enduring grandeur. Today one can create verse and call it poetry by doing a Google search, then blending the results into lines of absurdity. And, yes, it has a name: flarf. Flarf poetry and its derivatives have redefined what poetry is. Redefining is what postmodernity does best, and the result is that the rich literary legacy of the past is on the verge of being forgotten—and Watts with it.

Were he alive today, I doubt that it would occur to Watts to celebrate cyber randomness with his pen—or to write a hymn in celebration of himself. Watts was an extraordinarily gifted poet, one who virtually thought in rhyme and meter, and who wrote most of his poetry in first draft. With such skills, he could have been a leading man of letters in neo-classical Britain. Watts' era was termed the Age of Johnson, and Samuel Johnson himself ranked Watts among the great authors and said of him, "His ear was well tuned, and his diction was elegant and copious."[10]

Though the University of Edinburgh and the University of Aberdeen conferred on Watts the honor of doctor of divinity degrees in 1728, many literary critics have considered his poetry to be too explicitly Christian for literary acclaim. This was by design. Brilliant poet that he was, Watts avoided, as he termed it, the "excess baggage of intricate form as well as of poetical adornment."[11] His was a gospel objective first and last. Poetry, for Watts, was a means to a higher end, perhaps a requirement of all great poetry.

Hence, he was unapologetically a biblical and theological poet who has given to all Christians a rich legacy of sung worship, full of imagination, skill, deep theological perception, vivid sensory insight, cheerfulness in the midst of suffering and disadvantages, and a contagious sense of wonder at the majesty of God. Ours is a world that desperately needs Watts' poetry.

Second, we need Watts' voice in our worship. Christian worship desperately needs Watts. I have recently sat in worship services with well-meaning Christians singing, "Yes, Lord, yes, Lord, yes, yes, Lord." In another service, I sat bewildered as all around me folks held their hands aloft, caressing the air, singing, "Just think about it, just think about it, just think about it." Not wanting to stand there being the critic, I attempted to get my mind around just what it was I was supposed to be thinking about. Try as I might, I could find little in the vacuous lyrics they were crooning that required any degree of thought about anything.

I pity a world without Watts. I pity a church without him. Why would Christians want to cut themselves off from rich theological passion skillfully adorned, as in Watts' finest hymns?

In yet another service, I watched others sing Watts' "When I Survey the Wondrous Cross," but I was little moved by the words. As near as I can tell, the reason Watts did not move me this time was that there were many elements in that worship that distracted me from taking the words on my lips and into my heart as my own in singing them. The swaying worship leaders and all the paraphernalia of the indie-rock band filled the stage, and the volume was cranked up so loud that I was eventually forced to take my seven-year-old out of the place, his hands clamped tightly over his ears. I watched rather than sang because in this kind of entertainment venue, it matters little whether the congregation participates in the singing. It's fine if they do, of course, but it makes no difference to what one hears. The emotive vocal inflections and the pinched facial contortions of the well-meaning worship leader are difficult for most of us to emulate, and the occasional unexpected repetition of lines or addition of improvised lyrics leaves one singing something other than what the worship leader is singing. Not to worry, no one will hear you anyway.

I stood next to my eldest son in an urban warehouse church in Seattle, Washington, the walls painted black, various colored lighting flashing around the stage and room, the videographer projecting on the screen behind the band a giant close-up of the lead guitarist's fingers sliding up and down the neck of his instrument. Under the assaulting influence of the new nightclub liturgy, I again wondered whether I was supposed to be singing something. There were two thousand nineteen- to twenty-nine-year-olds in the room, but I could not hear anyone singing except the lead guitarist, and he was groaning in a manner I felt intensely uncomfortable attempting to emulate. I turned to my son, took a deep breath, and yelled, "Are we supposed to be singing?" He turned and hollered back in my ear, "I don't know." No one around us was disturbed in the slightest by our exchange.

Just as the medieval church cut off the congregation from participating in the sung worship of the service, today many well-meaning Christian leaders have reconstructed a sung worship wherein congregational participation does not matter. We sit or stand as our medieval forbears did and watch others sing for us. Worship has become a show, amusement, an entertaining means of connecting to the hip youth culture with, ostensibly, the gospel. Such a venue produces a response in the hearer—one super-charged with raw emotion—but I wonder whether it is an emotional response produced by a mind renewed by deep consideration of the objective truths of the gospel of grace or by the music itself.

Watts clearly understood all this. He no doubt learned it from the Psalms and perhaps from John Calvin's preface to his commentary on the Psalms:

We know by experience that singing has great force and vigor to move and inflame the hearts of men to invoke and praise God with a more vehement and ardent zeal. Care must always be taken that the song be neither light nor frivolous; but that it have weight and majesty (as St. Augustine says), and also, there is a great difference between music which one makes to entertain men at table and in their houses, and the Psalms which are sung in the Church in the presence of God and his angels.[12]

In an age of entertainment-driven worship, a recovered appreciation of Watts as a hymn writer is critical to correcting the "light" and "frivolous" tendencies of the postmodern church, and perhaps the dark and edgy ones, too. Every biblically mature generation in the church will want to contribute poetry and music to the church's worship—but, alas, so will every biblically immature one. Watts makes an excellent role model to guide the new generations of poets who presume to write lyrics for the corporate worship of God's people.

Instead of letting his son be guided by the transient poetic and music appetites of the moment, Watts' father taught him who must guide his pen:

> In ancient times God's worship did accord,
> Not with tradition, but the written word;
> Himself has told us how He'll be adored.[13]

Watts got his father's message: what Christians sing in worship must be guided by what God has revealed about how we are to sing to such a God. Watts mastered the poetic gift with which he was entrusted and earned the undisputed title "the Father of English Hymnody." If hymns are poems written in praise and adoration of God, then that makes Watts the father of English-speaking praise of God. Every Christian who cares about living a life of praise will want his sung worship to be guided by Watts' heart, mind, and poetic devotion. Why? Because Watts was consumed with wonder at Jesus Christ, the supreme object of Christian worship.

Third, we need Watts' example as we live in our frailty. Yet another important reason for surveying Watts' life and work is that his life is a model of patience in affliction for all Christians who suffer. The first years of his life were ones of constant political struggle, uncertainty, and persecution, during which his father was in and out of prison for his faith in Christ. All of his seventy-four years were ones of overcoming great difficulties. Watts was chronically ill throughout much of his adult life, suffering with a continual low-grade fever and often enduring intense physical discomfort.

Moreover, Watts lived with inescapable personal unattractiveness. Put bluntly, he was not a handsome man. This is big for Americans, who spend $15 billion a year on cosmetic surgery—one hundred times the entire annual gross domestic product of Uganda. We might dismiss the significance of his ugliness by assuming his society did not care about such frivolities. But it did. Perhaps next only to our own, people in the Enlightenment were profoundly preoccupied with physical appearance and adornment, including ridiculously elaborate wigs, male make-up, and pink satin culottes—for men. In our therapeutic culture, Watts would be a candidate for insecurity and a life of low self-esteem. Today his doctor would prescribe counseling, perhaps a regimen of anti-depressant drugs—and a face-lift.

Furthermore, Watts held religious views that were the mockery of the elite in his society, and he made the unforgiveable social blunder of not attending the right schools. As a Nonconformist, he was unwelcome at Oxford and Cambridge, and was forced to attend small, insignificant institutions, under the censure and scorn of a refined society.

We need Watts for many reasons. We need his poetry to aid us in recovering a sanctified understanding and imagination. We need him to help reform worship and singing in our churches today. And all of us who have ever felt marginalized for our frailty, our unattractiveness, our lack of formal learning in elite schools, or for any other limitation—real or perceived—need Watts. All people will find a wealth of enrichment and encouragement by learning more of the poetic wonder of Isaac Watts.

CHAPTER ONE

Watts' Life and Legacy

Born July 17, 1674,[1] Isaac Watts entered a deeply troubled Britain. Eleven years before his birth, a horrific outbreak of the bubonic plague swept through London, killing more than one hundred thousand people. Watts' birthplace, the port city of Southampton, was nearly depopulated by the same outbreak; streets were deserted and overgrown with weeds. The following year, all England was devastated at the news of the Great Fire leveling much of the capital city.

But disease and disaster were not the only afflictions on Britain at the time of Watts' birth. The nation was still struggling through massive, interrelated religious and political upheavals.

PERSECUTION

Earlier in the century, Roman Catholic-friendly Stuart monarchs had begun to assert their divine right and to rule as absolutists over both state and church. Puritans and Separatists who were able fled to the American colonies for religious freedom. After centuries of monarchial rule limited by a representative Parliament, it was inevitable that king and Parliament would come to blows. In 1642, King Charles I engaged in a bloody civil war with Parliament, ending with the defeat of the royalists and the beheading of the monarch. Lord Protector Oliver Cromwell commenced efforts to unite the country but found himself at odds with Presbyterian Scotland, with which he fought another civil war.

Finally, in 1660, Parliament invited Charles' son to assume the throne as King Charles II, restoring the monarchy. Charles promptly asserted his divine right and began a wholesale persecution of Nonconformists (Christians who refused to worship according to the dictates of the Anglican Church) throughout the realm. With the Act of Uniformity in 1662, Charles determined to reclaim his headship of the Anglican Church, the church everyone in his realm was required to attend. For refusing to acknowledge the king as head over the church, and for failing to be licensed to preach by the local bishop, John Bunyan, author of *The Pilgrim's Progress*, was imprisoned for twelve years, and many other ministers suffered the same fate. Charles II's policies, carried on by his brother, James II, led to the deaths of more than eighteen thousand Scottish Covenanters, who refused to bow to the usurper of the "Crown Rights of the Redeemer in His Kirk."[2]

Troubles far away are easily endured, but these troubles were at the Watts family's door. Isaac Watts Sr. was a Nonconformist deacon at the Above Bar Congregational Chapel in Southampton, where Rev. Nathanael Robinson was the pastor. When Watts was born, his father was serving a second term in prison for failing to conform to the Anglican Church. His mother, Sarah Taunton, would sit on a stone mounting block in front of the prison and nurse the newborn Isaac while talking with her husband through the bars. Sarah, "a pious woman, and a woman of taste,"[3] was the daughter of Alderman Taunton, whose ancestors had escaped, along with many other French Protestants (the Huguenots), to Southampton after the St. Bartholomew's Day Massacre in 1572. In 1685, when Watts was eleven, another wave of Huguenots immigrated to England with the revocation of the Edict of Nantes by French King Louis XIV and the restoration of state persecution of French Calvinists. The Watts family lived at 41 French Street, surrounded by Huguenot Christians whose families had suffered persecution for generations.[4]

Determined to bring Nonconformists to heel, the king and Parliament had implemented escalating penalties for those who refused to attend Anglican services, though these could be implemented arbitrarily. First came monetary fines, which often exceeded the entire annual incomes of families. Then followed the seizure of land and property; imprisonment; banishment and exile; and, finally, death by hanging. Married only one year, the elder Watts had been arbitrarily imprisoned for his Nonconformity when Sarah gave birth to Isaac, the first of their eight children. It would not be his last time behind bars.[5]

A FATHER'S INFLUENCE

When not in prison, Watts' father, a clothier by trade, conducted a boarding school in their home. Politicians and elitists today like to tar Christians as ignorant, uneducated roughs; rarely a fair representation at any time, it was certainly false in Watts' day. Nonconformist learning was rigorous, and the Watts' home school developed such a reputation for academic excellence that students came from as far away as America and the West Indies to study under the tutelage of the elder Isaac Watts.[6]

Watts Sr. took great care that his children should not be embittered against God because of his suffering. He told them, "Do not entertain any hard thoughts of God or of His ways, because His people are persecuted for them; for Jesus Christ Himself was persecuted to death by wicked men, for preaching the truth and doing good; and the holy apostles and prophets were cruelly used for serving God in His own way."[7] During a lull in persecution, Watts Sr. was freed and began teaching his son Latin when he was only four years old. While still a young man, Watts would go on to master Greek, Hebrew, and French.

In a letter to his children on May 21, 1685, during a forced exile in London, Watts Sr. gave careful guidance concerning distortions of the gospel imposed by the Anglo-Catholic established church:

> Worship God in His own way, with true worship and in a right manner, according to the rules of the gospel, and not according to the inventions or traditions of men. Consider, that idolatry and superstition are both abominable to God. Now idolatry is the worshipping of idols, images, pictures, crucifixes, and consecrated bread, as the papists do, and no idolaters must enter into heaven. Superstition is to make additions of ordinances or ceremonies to God's worship more than He hath appointed. Take heed, my children, of these things. It is not enough to say that such things are not forbidden in Scripture; but you must see whether they are commanded there, or else obey them not.[8]

Watts Sr.'s earnest instruction in his letter gives considerable insight into the ways in which Roman Catholicism persisted in Anglican worship and why he was willing to suffer persecution rather than conform to it. He continued:

> Entertain not in your hearts any of the popish doctrines, of having more mediators than one, namely, the Lord Jesus; of praying to the Virgin Mary, or any other

saints or angels; for saints and angels, though in heaven, yet they are creatures; and prayer is a divine worship due to none but God the Father, Son, and Spirit.[9]

Watts Sr. did not want his children deceived by a creeping distortion of justification by grace alone through faith alone in Christ alone: "Avoid their doctrine of meriting by works of obedience, for there is some sin that pollutes our best duties, and we can deserve nothing at God's hand but wrath. All the good we receive comes of His free grace." He described other "erroneous and damnable doctrines," and concluded, "You must receive no doctrine, but such as is rightly built upon the Holy Scriptures," a theme Watts would often hear in his formative years. He closed the letter with an exhortation for his loved ones to discern the truth and to prepare for suffering: "My children, pray to God to give you the knowledge of the truth, and to keep you from error, for it is a very dangerous time you are like to live in."[10]

CHILD POET

Poetry played a more central role in academic learning in Watts' day, and the Watts family had excelled in it for generations. Isaac Watts' grandfather, captain of a British warship who was eventually killed during a sea battle with the Dutch, often wrote poetry, and he passed the love of it on to his son. His widow, Watts' grandmother, played an important role in Watts' early nurture in the things of God. Watts' father, a man of settled Nonconformist convictions, tutored his son in both poetry and biblical worship of God, unadulterated by superstitious traditions held over from pre-Reformation England. Watts Sr. vented his frustration at the established church in a couplet:

Why do our churchmen with such zeal contend
For what the Scriptures nowhere recommend?[11]

An early instance of young Watts' poetic inclination came one evening during family worship at the dinner table. While his father read Scripture and guided family prayers, Watts spotted a mouse climbing up the bell pull and began to giggle. Rebuked by his father, who asked him why he was laughing during prayer, Watts replied:

There was mouse for want of stairs
Ran up a rope to say his prayers.[12]

His parents, amazed at the boy's ability to rhyme in his head without writing the lines down on paper, encouraged his rhyming—for a while. As children will do when encouraged, Watts began rhyming all the time. Annoyed by the incessant rhyming, his father forbade him to do it—and he meant it. Isaac soon forgot and fell back into rhyming. Taking him over his knees, Watts Sr. prepared to lay into his son's backside with the switch. Then young Watts rather unconvincingly cried:

O father, do some mercy take,
And I will no more verses make.[13]

His father did some mercy take that day, but the church can be grateful that Watts, contrary to his childish resolve, continued to make verses throughout the remainder of his life. The very gift that so annoyed his parents when he was a child would be sanctified and become the means of enriching the worship of tens of thousands of Christians in his lifetime, and millions in the centuries since his death.

Watts' mother, Sarah, found some handwritten poems one day and asked whether they were Isaac's. He claimed they were his, but she doubted that a child could write poetry with the degree of depth she observed. An idea occurred to her, and she promptly had her son sit down at the kitchen table and write her a poem. He did. Note the depth of his gospel understanding in these ten lines written on demand when he was seven years old:

I am a vile polluted lump of earth;
So I've continued since my birth;
Although Jehovah grace does daily give me,
As sure this monster Satan will deceive me.
Come, therefore, Lord, from Satan's claws relieve me.

Wash me in Thy blood, O Christ,
And grace divine impart.

Then search and try the corners of my heart,
That I in all things may be fit to do
Service to Thee, and sing Thy praises too.[14]

Young Watts needed ten lines because he chose to write a poem that not only would rhyme but would also be an acrostic on his name, "Isaac Watts," which has ten letters. This was, no doubt, one of those moments that a mother cherishes and hides up in her heart. Imagine Sarah Watts' wonder at her son's gifting, but still more, the gratitude to God any Christian mother would have for so obvious a working of grace in her son's heart.

BOOKS AND THE BOOK

While still younger than the age when most children begin school today, Watts showed a passion for books and learning. When any amount of money came his way, he would run to his mother, exclaiming: "A book, a book! Buy me a book!"[15] However, widely learned as his father was, he instructed his eldest son and all his children "frequently to read the Scriptures—get your hearts to delight in them—above all books and writings account the Bible the best and read it most— lay up the truth of it in your hearts." And lest they become too enamored with the world's wisdom, he taught them, "Let all the knowledge and learning you attain by other books, both at school and at home, be improved as servants to help you the better to understand God's Word. The sum of all the counsel I can give you is contained in that blessed Word of God."[16] Guided by such a Bible-centered father, Watts as a youth came to love the Word of God and to love all those who loved God's Word.

At the Nonconformist gatherings, prayer and expository preaching from the Bible were central features of the service. The sermons of Robinson that Watts listened to as a youth were studied, theological, and careful exhortations—and they were long. Shallow homilies might do in the established church, but Nonconformist Christians came together expecting to get at the meat of the text. In a day when sermons have become pedantic lectures or therapeutic chats, we might be tempted to think these sermons were dull and boring. The singing would have appeared so to most—as it did to young Watts—but the preaching was delivered with passion so that it came home to the conscience.[17]

Those who pray, worship, and are persecuted together form particularly strong bonds. The Watts family expanded into a much larger one each Lord's Day as they gathered at the independent chapel, surrounded by friends and neighbors who were fellow suffering members of the family of God's faithful. Watts may have been thinking of his father, Robinson, or any number of other "men of heavenly birth" with whom he worshiped when he penned this quatrain:

Let others choose the sons of mirth,
To give a relish to their wine;

I love the men of heavenly birth,
Whose thoughts and language are divine.[18]

While still a boy, Watts here encapsulated his resolve, by the grace of God, not to be an enemy of Christ by making intimate friendship with the world (James 4:4). As a result, the subsequent decades of his life were remarkably fruitful in the service of Christ and His kingdom.

TEEN YEARS AND FIRST HYMN

Most parents are convinced that their children are above average, even precocious. Who hasn't seen family minivans placarded with bumper stickers that announce, "My child is an honor student at such-and-such school"? Isaac Watts Sr. would not have had the equivalent on his family's horse-drawn buggy, but he knew that his son had been endowed by the grace of God with unique academic and creative gifts; that his son was, in fact, precocious. Desiring the best academic education for young Isaac, Watts Sr. decided to send him to the Free School in Southampton. That may seem normal, but it would be comparable today to a Baptist father sending his son to a Jesuit school. Watts was a Nonconformist, but the Free School, later called King Edward VI School, was Anglican. Rev. John Pinhorne, a one-time vicar of the Anglican parish church in Eling, was master of the school. For Watts Sr., sending his son to the Anglicans for education was potentially sending him to consort with the "sons of mirth."[19]

But it was not to be so. Pinhorne proved to be not only an able teacher of the classics but an earnest Christian who urged all of his students to develop their minds and understandings for the honor of Christ throughout their lives. In this, Pinhorne reinforced Watts Sr.'s instruction to his son: "Learn to know God, especially learn to know him in and through the Lord Jesus Christ and to be acquainted with this blessed Redeemer of God's elect."[20]

Over the next years, Watts mastered Latin, Greek, Hebrew, and French under Pinhorne's instruction. With respect and affection, Watts wrote his "Pindaric Ode" to pay honor to his tutor and to express the "debt of thanks" he owed him. After rehearsing "Plato's walks" and "Latium's fields," Watts wrote that he despised Zeus, "The fabled ruler of the skies." He then proceeded to "consecrate his lays," or to map out the "numbers" or metered lines of his poetic life's work:

Thy name. Almighty Sire, and thine,
Jesus, where His full glories shine,
Shall consecrate my lays;
In numbers, by no vulgar bounds controlled,
In numbers, most divinely strong and bold,
I'll sound through all the world th' immeasurable praise.[21]

While under Pinhorne's tutelage, Watts wrote in his personal memoranda of important events in his life: "Fell under considerable convictions of sin, 1688, and was taught to trust in Christ I hope, 1689." In the latter year, he also wrote that he "had a great and dangerous sickness,"[22] one that had lingering effects throughout the remainder of his years. Through all this, Watts excelled in both piety and learning, and for his academic success and poetic ability became somewhat the talk of Southampton. Daily nurture in Scripture as he grew in knowledge prevented Watts from developing the pride so common to all, but perhaps especially to those endowed with considerable gifts. Hence, there was no hint of vanity in him at the adulations of the community.

THE OFFER

In 1690, Southampton physician Dr. John Speed began developing an interest in young Watts' education. He discussed Watts with other men of means in the community and made a proposal. These men would pay for Watts to go to Oxford or Cambridge, there to prepare for the Christian ministry. For Watts, it was like receiving an offer of a full-ride scholarship to his choice of the finest universities in the realm. But there was a catch. Dr. Speed was an Anglican. Oxford and Cambridge were Anglican. To study at these institutions in Watts' day, one had to be an Anglican. Accepting the offer meant converting to Anglicanism, which meant rejecting his father's Nonconformity.

Watts was a sixteen-year-old young man who had been raised in a Nonconformist home that would be considered strict and authoritarian by today's standards. He was being given an opportunity to launch out on his own, to feel his independence, and to be his own man. What's more, he had seen in his respected teacher, Pinhorne, a man who was both a true Christian and an Anglican. What would young Watts do? I wonder what Watts Sr. was thinking and praying in those days. "I remember you always with myself in my daily prayers addressed to the throne of grace,"[23] he once wrote from prison to his son.

The love and nurture of Watts' godly father won out, and he graciously declined Dr. Speed's offer, "determined to take his lot among the dissenters."[24] He later wrote lines in one of his hymns that express the kind of resolve he drew upon at this turning point in his life and academic career:

> I'm not ashamed to own my Lord
> Or to defend his cause,
> Maintain the honor of his Word,
> The glory of his cross.[25]

TEENAGE HYMN

Though there was life and passion in the praying and the preaching at the Nonconformist chapel in Southampton, the singing was, at best, awkward and uninspiring. The Anglicans and the Nonconformists were fully agreed upon the importance of singing in worship. The inspired psalms were the finest poetry ever penned, and Hebrew worshipers took on their lips the highest poetic expressions as they sang to God, but in Watts' day, many psalm versifications fell considerably short of fine poetry. In their sincere efforts to strictly reproduce the inspired text, most versifiers paid less attention to beauty of expression. Poet that he was becoming, this offended young Watts.

Hymnologist Erik Routley writes that "Watts protested against the dullness and crudity of expression" of the poetry that was sung in worship and was "offended by the gawkiness of Barton's Psalms." Watts himself put it this way: "The singing of God's praise is the part of worship nighest heaven, but its performance among us is the worst on earth."[26]

One Sunday in 1690, as the Watts family strolled home after worship, sixteen-year-old Isaac made a comment about the singing. He referred to what they had just sung as "ugly hymns." Watts Sr. halted and rebuked his son: "If you do not like the hymns, young man, then give us something better."[27]

That afternoon, Watts sharpened his quill and wrote a hymn of eight stanzas drawing loosely from Revelation 5:6–12. It began:

Behold the glories of the Lamb,
Amidst His Father's throne;
Prepare new honors for His name,
And songs before unknown.[28]

With this opening quatrain, young Watts was unknowingly mapping out the poetic contribution, "prepar[ing] new honors" in song for the Lamb, that would occupy his pen throughout the remaining years of his life. In the final seven stanzas of the hymn, he explored the rest of the prophetic text: the singing of a new song, the elders around the throne, the incense, the prayers of the saints, the taking up of the scroll, the worthiness and glories of the Son, the making of the people of God into kings and priests, and heaven and the saints' final reigning with God. Watts' ability as a poet would improve, though his remarkable debut effort clearly showed the biblical and theological understanding and the poetic skill necessary to craft "new songs" worthy of the Lamb.

When Watts came down the stairs a while later and presented his first hymn effort to his father, Watts Sr. was duly impressed and took a copy of it to the Independent chapel that evening. In 1690, in Southampton, England, the Above Bar congregation became the first to sing a hymn of Isaac Watts. It was enthusiastically received and Watts was encouraged to write more like it.[29] The Watts revolution in hymnody had begun.

STUDENT SCHOLAR

Watts' university education at Newington Academy would play an important role in preparing and equipping him for a life of doxology. There, sixteen-year-old Watts would encounter the soul-killing unbelief of the Age of Reason and be forced to grapple with reason and the Christian faith. Would cultured London ruin his soul? Or would he come to own personally the gospel of grace in Christ that had been taught in his home?

Leaving his home in Southampton in 1690 to begin his studies at the dissenting academy near London was a tearful event. Watts deeply loved his parents and his siblings, and he expressed his sadness in a poetic epistle he later sent home:

E'er since the morning of that day
Which bid my dearest friends adieu,
And rolling wheels bore me away
Far from my native town and you,
E'er since I lost through distant place,
The pleasures of a parent's face. . . .[30]

He continued, describing his letter as "Laden with humble love" and as a sort of long-distance kiss to them.[31] Perhaps Watts was not unlike a young man today leaving to go off to college, his twinges of homesickness and longing for family shouted down by the anticipated adventure of independence and college life.

Watts wrote briefly of this new stage in his life in his personal memoranda: "1690, left the grammar-school, and came to London to Mr. Rowe's, to study philosophy."[32] Though the Anglican universities might have given him more grounding in mathematics and classics, Newington Academy, like other dissenting academies, tended to provide a more liberal, wide-ranging education, with greater emphasis on modern languages, history, and literature since the classics. But first and last, the academy was designed to prepare Watts for the ministry of the gospel.

The Rev. Thomas Rowe was director of the academy and the pastor of a Nonconformist congregation that met in Haberdasher's Hall, London. Watts soon became a member of his schoolmaster's congregation. The curriculum at the academy, where novelist Daniel Defoe had studied before him, was comprehensive: Watts studied Latin, Greek, Hebrew, mathematics, history, geography, natural science, rhetoric, ethics, metaphysics, anatomy, law, and theology. Students were expected to develop mastery of oral disputation and of written composition. They were regularly guided in carefully studying the Bible, outlining passages for sermons, and preparing lessons from the Psalms.

In this higher education, Watts was profoundly influenced by Rowe, "who was Calvinist in theology, Lockean in philosophy, and Cartesian in physics."[33] Rowe would influence Watts in all of these areas and is credited with contributing to Watts' understanding of Christianity as a "reasonable" religion, that is, one that is founded on supernatural revelation and not in contradiction to reason. Watts wrote a poetic tribute to this beloved teacher:

I love thy gentle influence, Rowe,
Thy gentle influence, like the sun,
Only dissolves the frozen snow,
Then bids our thoughts like rivers flow.[34]

REASON AND FAITH IN LONDON

When Watts arrived in London, Sir Isaac Newton was forty-eight years old and a celebrated man of science, and John Locke, the venerated empirical philosopher, was in his sixty-eighth year. London was the intellectual capital of the realm, if not of all Europe, and it was the Age of Reason.[35] Hence, young Watts' faith would have faced considerable philosophical challenges.

He approached learning with zeal, but also with modesty and humility. Yet he was frustrated with the new customs of education, the laws of learning that encouraged students to "rove without confinement," which he believed actually enchained students. Perhaps it was Watts' contemporary, Alexander Pope, who best laid out the educational theory Watts so disliked:

Know then thyself, presume not God to scan;
The proper study of mankind is man.[36]

Not so for Watts, or for his correspondent, the countess of Hertford, who wished that "a muse like Mr. Pope's were more inclined to exert itself on Divine subjects."[37] Ever the poet, Watts embodied his frustration with the tyranny of Enlightenment educational theory in lines of verse:

Custom, that tyranness of fools,
That leads the learned round the schools,

In magic chains of forms and rules!
My genius storms her throne . . .
I hate these shackles of the mind
Forg'd by the haughty wise.[38]

FRIENDSHIPS AND INFLUENCES

Watts developed lifelong friendships with some of his fellow students, including Samuel Say, whose Puritan father had been ejected from his pulpit in Southampton, and who would later encourage Watts to write an entirely new version of psalm versifications; Joseph Hort, who would become an Anglican bishop; and John Hughes, who would become a journalist, writing articles for Joseph Addison's London journal *The Spectator*. Hughes often said that men fail to make progress in learning not for lack of time or ability but for lack of hard work. Unlike so many university students today, who stay up late partying, eating pizza, and playing video games, Watts and his friends did not fritter away the hours. They did, however, stay up late. Far into the night, Watts went on reading and annotating what he read. Later in life, he realized with regret how doing this had irreversibly contributed to his poor health and insomnia. In one sermon he said, "Midnight studies are prejudicial to nature, and painful experience calls me to repent of the faults of my younger years."[39]

London in Watts' day was a city of great preachers, and he and his friends were determined to hear as many of them, and as often, as they could manage. Watts wrote of John Howe, the awe-invoking former chaplain to Oliver Cromwell; of Thomas Gouge, who preached at the meetinghouse on Thames Street; and of Joseph Stennett, preacher at Pinner's Hall and author of the hymn "O Blessed Savior, Is Thy Love." His grandson Samuel Stennett would author the better-known hymn "Majestic Sweetness Sits Enthroned"; both grandfather and grandson wrote on themes that would occupy Watts' pen as a hymn writer.[40]

OTHER TEEN WRITING

"Whatever he took in hand," wrote Samuel Johnson of Watts, "was by his incessant solitude for souls converted to theology."[41] The foundation for this single-minded inclination, as we have seen, came first from Watts' home and father, but it was significantly reinforced under Rowe's tutelage in these years. And Watts took much in hand. In 1691, when he was seventeen, Watts wrote a lyric poem to his brother Enoch titled *Going Avoyage*. He wrote a Latin letter in verse to his brother Richard, who would become a physician, and a number of other fine poems that would be published in 1706 in his collection of lyric poems titled *Horae Lyricae*.

After his death, twenty-two Latin essays were discovered that Watts must have written as exercises during his teen years at Rowe's academy in London. Of these essays, Johnson wrote, "These show a degree of knowledge, both philosophical and theological, such as very few attain by a much longer course of study."[42]

BACK HOME

In 1694, having become a twenty-year-old man of considerable learning and ability, Watts completed his studies in London and returned to Southampton and home. In his memoranda, he wrote: "I went into the country June, 1694. Dwelt at my father's house two years and a quarter." During this time, Watts principally studied Holy Scripture, taking all that he had learned from other books, as his father had instructed him, and employing his vast learning to one end—the earnest investigation of God's Word.[43] In a manner not unlike his contemporary Jonathan Edwards, Watts also took great pleasure in studying the natural world around him in Southampton. His sister wrote of how their older brother attempted to inspire in his younger siblings a love of creation, urging them to "look through nature" to the hand of the Almighty who had made all things and is glorified in them. The following lines reflect both his fascination with nature and his understanding of the limitation of natural revelation, and they reveal his longing for communion with Jesus, Creator God:

My God, I love and I adore:
But souls that love would know thee more.
Wilt thou for ever hide, and stand
Behind the labours of thy hand?

Thy hand unseen sustains the poles
On which this huge creation rolls. . . .

Beyond the golden morning-star!
Fain would I trace th'immortal way,
That leads to courts of endless day,
Where the Creator stands confess'd,
In His own fairest glories dress'd.
Some shining spirit help me rise,
Come waft a stranger through the skies;
Bless'd Jesus, meet me on the road,
First offspring of th'eternal God,
Thy hand shall lead a younger son,
Clothe me with vestures yet unknown,
And place me near my Father's throne.[44]

These two years were, no doubt, a critical time in Watts' young life: re-entering family life, re-establishing his relationship with his father, grappling and wrestling with Enlightenment ideas, sorting out what the Scriptures taught on many subjects, contemplating what he was to do with his life, and praying for divine guidance in the next stages.

Unknown to Watts, on the eve of the eighteenth century, the great age of doubt and skepticism, he was being readied by God to be the father of the great age of hymnody. As he worshiped with his family at Above Bar Congregational Chapel and grimaced at the singing of the awkward versions of the psalms, perhaps the following lines began forming in his mind:

Our lives through various scenes are drawn,
And vexed with trifling cares;
While thine eternal thought moves on
Thine undisturbed affairs.[45]

EDUCATOR AND PREACHER

In 1696, he was called to be a tutor in the home of the wealthy and influential Nonconformist John Hartopp. There, Watts learned a critical and rare skill: how to descend from the heights of philosophic investigation to the level of a child's understanding. During his work as a private tutor, Watts wrote his classic work on logic and continued writing hymns.[46]

On his twenty-fourth birthday, July 17, 1698, Watts was called upon to preach at Mark Lane Chapel, one of the most influential pulpits in London. The congregation, which had been shrinking under the inept ministry of Dr. Isaac Chauncey, took delight in the gentle but persuasively passionate preaching of the young man. Within a short time, he was called to preach every week, and attendance grew from seventy-four to more than five hundred in the years of his ministry.[47]

A LIFE OF DOXOLOGY

Throughout the rest of his life, Watts suffered a low-grade fever and various ailments, but in 1712 he became so sick that he was no longer able to preach. Invited to visit the palatial estate of Sir Thomas Abney, one-time lord mayor of London, Watts was kindly taken in by the family. What was intended to be a week of rest turned into thirty-six years. Productive years they were, with Watts writing more than fifty books on such diverse subjects as philosophy, mathematics, astronomy, and theology. These included an important treatise on prayer, a book on the importance and method of establishing Christian charity schools, a work on the use and abuse of the emotions in worship, and a dialogue wherein Watts soundly refutes Deism.

But Watts is best known and loved for his wonder expressed in his poetry. He is remembered for writing 750 hymns that appeared in several important publications during his lifetime. His first book of poetry was called *Horae Lyricae. Poems, Chiefly of the Lyric kind* (1706, expanded in 1709). Perhaps his best-known work, *Hymns and Spiritual Songs, In Three Books*, was published in 1707 and later expanded. His defining work for children, *Divine Songs Attempted in Easy Language for the Use of Children*, was published in 1715. Watts' controversial interpretation of the Psalms first appeared in 1719: *The Psalms of David Imitated in the Language of the New Testament, And apply'd to the Christian State and Worship*. The best of these poetic works justly earned Watts the title "the Father of English Hymnody."

Watts died peacefully on November 25, 1748, at his adopted home with the Abney family. He is buried at Bunhill Fields, the Nonconformist cemetery in London.[48]

Let us now look more closely at the stages of Watts life during which he wrote his hymns. As we do so, we will attempt to discover the circumstances and inspiration behind the wonder evident in the finest of his poetic works.

WATTS: A MODEL FOR THE AGES

As the church casts about, trying to find out how we should do church, how we should worship, and particularly how we should sing in our worship, Watts can provide us with a theological and poetic anchor. "The Father of English Hymnody" gives us the perfect combination that everyone in the church ought to be striving to reach: passion and feeling grounded on solid theological foundations.

Like few others through the ages, Watts gives us both the head and the heart of sung worship; he helps us both think and feel in our singing. For cerebral Christians who want the head but ignore the heart, Watts lays bare the heart of worship. For those who want the heart but ignore the head, Watts winsomely adorns the beauty of doctrinal purity; he reveals the theological foundations of the gospel in rich ways that renew our minds and awaken heartfelt gratitude and love for the Savior.

My hope and prayer is that this study of Watts' life will be known and felt to be intensely relevant to what *and* how we are to sing in worship today and throughout the ages.

Chapter Two

Watts as Educator

Anyone who has ever been unemployed will appreciate the tendency to gut-wrenching anxiety that must have tempted Watts during the more than two years he spent at home after completing his college education. Unlike many under similar circumstances, however, Watts seems to have spent much less time gnawing his nails and far more time praying and studying his Bible.

Just when he may have begun to wonder whether God had a role for him, whether he would ever get a job, a letter arrived. He was offered a position as a private tutor to the only son and six daughters of Sir John Hartopp and his wife, Elizabeth. Accordingly, on October 15, 1696, Watts made his way back to Newington. His time in the Hartopps' godly London home would add another formative layer in his preparation for his life's work: crafting hymns for all Christians to sing to God in corporate worship.

In his new employment, Watts was, in effect, taken under the patronage of a wealthy and influential family. Here he would be forced to make all his learning accessible and practical as he taught the children, and he would once again be in the circle of the most prominent preachers of the day. What is more, in this arrangement he would have time to continue his studies and writing.

The Hartopp home, for all its wealth and influence, was first and last a Christian home, led by a deeply devout Christian man. Watts wrote of him:

> When I name Sir John Hartopp all that knew him will agree that I name a gentleman, a scholar, and a Christian. He had a taste for universal learning. But the Book of God was his chief study and his divinest delight; his Bible lay before him night and day . . . his doors were ever open, and his carriage was always friendly and courteous to the ministers of the Gospel. He was a present refuge for the oppressed. He often entertained his family in the evening worship on the Lord's Day with excellent discourses.[1]

Watts described how, during these discourses, the venerable patriarch of the Hartopp home at times was overcome with emotion as he spoke of the grace of the gospel. His eyes would tear up and his "voice would be interrupted, and there would be a sacred pause and silence."[2]

Though Watts would mark July 17, 1698, his twenty-fourth birthday, as the first time he publicly preached a sermon before a sophisticated London congregation, evidence suggests that Hartopp called on him to deliver discourses on the Word of God before the Hartopp family. But his daily work was that of teaching children. Brilliant scholar that he had become, Watts loved teaching children. There was nothing of drudgery in his duties to young John Hartopp and his sisters. Rather, he thought of teaching as a noble calling and wrote, "How lovely is it to see a teacher waiting upon those that are slow of understanding, and taking due time and pains to make the learner conceive what he means without upbraiding him with his weakness."[3]

Before a gathering of schoolteachers, Watts urged them to show the beauty of the Christian gospel in all their instruction:

Youth is the time of acquiring knowledge, and as you have the important charge laid upon you of instructing some of the rising generation, let me beg that you will leave nothing undone to make your pupils love the beauties of religion. Teach them that religion has nothing in it of a gloomy nature, for how can that be gloomy that leads to everlasting pleasures?[4]

The more one reads Watts and other Puritans, the more baffling is the persistent caricature of Puritanism as a dour, frowning religion. The misrepresentation was perpetrated by men such as journalist H. L. Mencken, who defined Puritanism as "The haunting fear that someone, somewhere, may be happy."[5] Such deconstructing fails to reckon with the Puritan Watts' cheerful piety, as seen throughout his life and writing.

Early Writings

Watts' years as a teacher of children would be invaluable to him in writing his *Divine Songs for Children* and in his preaching before a congregation that was made up of many children. As he taught the Hartopp children, he also developed a guide to teaching language arts: grammar, writing, reading, and interpreting literature; it was published in 1721 as *The Art of Reading and Writing English*. In between lessons with the children, he also wrote significant portions of his work *Improvement of the Mind*, in which he argued, among other things, for regular and systematic memorization of literature, but especially of Holy Scripture.[6]

Watts also continued with his investigations of weighty philosophical matters, especially ones related to epistemology, the study of how knowledge is acquired. The result was that during these years of tutoring, Watts wrote a defining book on logic, which he dedicated to his students' father, Sir John Hartopp. The book, titled *Logic, The Right Use of Reason in the Inquiry After Truth* and published in 1724, ironically became the standard text on the subject at Oxford and Cambridge,[7] institutions that refused to admit a Nonconformist such as Watts.

By "logic," Watts did not mean the clever trickery of rhetorical argument, whereby flawed views were made to appear true. He used the word *logic* in this negative way in a translation from the Latin of another poet, wherein Watts criticized the established church, which he termed:

> *A warrior well furnish'd*
> *With all arts politic and polite,*
> *With the knotty embarrassments of criticism,*
> *The hampering chains and subtleties of logic,*
> *And the javelins of pen and tongue,*
> *With the roaring ordinance of councils and canons,*
> *And all the artillery of the schools and gown.*[8]

In his *Logic*, Watts was interested in breaking the "hampering chains and subtleties," and thereby equipping his students to take "captive every thought to make it obedient to Christ." Watts deeply disliked the "noisy and furious contests" in which "several factions" of Christians were engaged in his day, and he despised oratory that was used to conceal truth and to obscure the real questions under discussion. "I am very unwilling to contend in a dispute. Sophistry and oratory throw so much paint upon the question in dispute, or raise so much dust about it, as to conceal the truth from the eye of the mind, and hide the merits of the cause from reason."[9]

God did not intend for men to use the mind and the tongue as a means of throwing paint at and raising dust on the reason. In *Logic*, Watts set out to give his students the rational skills to make clear what he believed others labored to obscure. His teaching method is seen in what he wrote about logic's role in acquiring truth: "*Veritas in puteo*," that is, "Truth lies in a well." He added, "Logic suppl[ies] us with steps whereby we may go down to reach the water."[10] The formal study of logic has fallen on hard times in our world. But those who master Watts' *Logic* will be far better equipped to unmask bad thinking, to see the Devil's schemes before they hit. Watts argued that studying logic helps a man expose the "disguise and false colors in which many things appear to us in this present imperfect state."[11]

CUTTING THROUGH DECEPTION

For Watts, studying logic was no mere academic exercise, engaged in as an end in itself. Since Satan is in the business of deception, Watts wrote that it is the Devil's strategy that "knavery puts on the face of justice; deceit and evil are often clothed in the shapes and appearances of truth and goodness." Watts saw logic as a way of aiding men in unmasking the deception: "Logic helps us strip off the outward disguise of things, and to behold and judge them in their own nature."[12]

One wonders what satirical verse Watts would write about the knavery of the media, politicians, and educational elites who make it their daily business to defy logic and reasonable discourse. Consider, for example, *New York Times* columnist Anthony Lewis' declarative conclusion about people, such as Christians, who believe there are things about which we can and should be absolutely certain: "Certainty is the enemy of decency and humanity."[13] Watts, no doubt, would guide young John Hartopp in explicating the flawed logic used by this leading American journalist. He would expose the basic problem with the skeptic Lewis' absolutist declaration: he is *certain* he is right about the evils of certainty.

Watts' *Logic* will aid young people in learning to see through the absurdity of amoralists who claim to hold the intellectual high ground, but who must borrow arguments from moral absolutists to defend their territory. Watts would be gracious, I'm certain, but he would have little time for those who make absolutist statements condemning people for being absolutists. He would likely write:

> *I hate these shackles of the mind*
> *Forg'd by the haughty wise.*[14]

He no doubt would have agreed with a far better Lewis—C. S. Lewis—who, in his Narnia classic *The Lion, the Witch and the Wardrobe*, has the professor fulminate at the cluttered thinking of the Pevensie children: "Logic! Why don't they teach logic at these schools?"[15] Watts agreed, and produced a perennial classic on logic, recently republished and available to aid a new generation in mastering the art of clear thinking.

In the midst of these happy and productive years of teaching, study, and writing in the Hartopp home, Watts began forming a plan to completely rewrite the Psalms in verse, and under the sanctifying influence of that godly Puritan home he was further equipped for his years of pastoral ministry, preaching, and crafting hymns.

WATTS: A HIGH VIEW OF SINGING

We may be tempted to dismiss a man of such brilliance, of such academic genius. How can Watts be relevant to our lives? How can a man writing the definitive book on logic speak to our age? Won't he be all head and no heart?

But observe how Watts was shaped by his calling as an educator. We tend to think that students are learners, while educators already know it all. This is a significant mistake. Watts' providential calling as a tutor of a small handful of children in one household was a means of shaping and honing his knowledge of how his mind worked, and of how other people's minds worked—in this case, children's minds. This would be essential learning for his future calling.

So it is with all of us. Whatever our gifts and callings, they are of very little use without right knowledge of ourselves and others.

Though he may not have fully understood it at the time, Watts as a teacher was being readied for his hymnological legacy. He may have found himself impatient with the squirming immaturity of the Hartopp children, frustrated and discouraged with their halting progress. But then, by the grace of God, his imagination came up with a plan to draw a poetic picture, to charm them with an imaginative comparison so that they could apprehend the knowledge he wanted to convey to them. That is precisely what Watts would later do so meaningfully and effectively in his poetry.

Though few of us are gifted and called as Watts was to begin a revolution in Christian singing in worship, all of us are being shaped by the fatherly care and wise providence of our loving heavenly Father. As with Watts, God has a role for each of us in the body of Christ and in the world. Whatever frustrations we encounter in the stages of our lives, as with Watts, God is there, working out His perfect plan to prepare us for our callings and for the trials ahead in those callings.

In the next stage of Watts' life, he would face one of his most grinding trials, and find grace to help in his time of need, grace that produced enduring beauty in his poetry.

CHAPTER THREE

Watts' Sermon Hymns

"I had rather be the author of Mr. [Richard] Baxter's *Call to the Unconverted*," wrote Isaac Watts, "than the author of [John] Milton's *Paradise Lost*."[1] For a man of letters, a poet often compared with Milton, Watts here beautifully clarifies his priorities as both a preacher and a poet.

While living and teaching in the Hartopp home, Watts became familiar with the Nonconformist congregation on Mark Lane, London. Today, Mark Lane is a street near the Tower of London lined mostly with architecturally bland twentieth-century buildings, but in Watts' day it was part of a fashionable district made up of the fine estates of wine and corn merchants. Watts' contemporary, the celebrated diarist Samuel Pepys, who was "writing a history without knowing it,"[2] was a regular member of high London society in the homes on Mark Lane.

The pulpit of Mark Lane Chapel had been occupied by some of the most eminent men in seventeenth-century England, under whom the congregation had flourished and grown. Westminster divine Joseph Caryl, who died the year before Watts was born, had started the church and been succeeded by John Owen, "the Calvin of England." Westminster Confession commentator David Clarkson followed Owen, and then came Dr. Isaac Chauncey. It has been said that for Chauncey's "dullness in the pulpit and his tactlessness out of it,"[3] Mark Lane, which had so long enjoyed the best of Puritan preachers, began to decline.

Watts had begun gaining experience in the pulpit. He had preached in the parish church in Freeby, Leicestershire, where the Hartopps kept a country home, and he also had preached at Above Bar Chapel in Southampton, the congregation of his childhood.

One Lord's Day when Watts was attending services at Mark Lane Chapel with the Hartopps, Sir John introduced him to the congregation. As a result, Watts was eventually asked to preach to this influential London congregation, as it turned out, on his twenty-fourth birthday. His message was enthusiastically received and he was asked to preach again. Perhaps Dr. Chauncey was a better physician than he was pastor and preacher.

Matters worsened when a controversy arose about the

nature of church discipline, during which Watts was asked to preach yet again. In 1698, Watts was asked to replace the assistant pastor, who was retiring. Soon Watts was preaching nearly every Sunday morning, while Chauncey continued preaching in the afternoon.[4] Watts was never heard to criticize his senior minister, and from him he gained a lasting connection to the American Colonies, where Chauncey's father had been president of Harvard from 1654–1671. As a result of this connection, Watts carried on a lifelong correspondence with Cotton Mather and other Colonial ministers.[5]

SERMON HYMNS

When Chauncey at last resigned in April 1701, the congregation had dwindled to less than half its former numbers. However, Watts preached with fresh expository skill, and his knowledge of Scripture enabled him to give the flock a comprehensive and unified message of the gospel of grace. Moreover, his knowledge of and love for children, combined with his fertile imagination, enabled him to capture the attention and the consciences of both young and old sitting under his preaching.

Watts was hindered, however, by chronic health problems. In May, he left London for Bath and then for his home in Southampton, hoping thereby to regain his strength. Many in the congregation at Mark Lane feared he would be unable to return. But in November, somewhat recovered, he came back.

On January 14, 1702, the congregation, "with one consent," asked Watts to be their minister. But Watts put them off and "urged them to fix on one who might more constantly preach amongst them twice a day,"[6] which, he argued, his health would not permit him to do. He made many other objections that the leadership of the church attempted to refute. This went on for some months, with Watts even suggesting three other men who he was sure would do a better job. Finally, ashamed at his own persistence in refusing their pleas, he wrote them:

> Your perseverance in your choice and love, your constant profession of edification by my ministry, the great probability you show me of building up this famous and decayed church of Christ if I accept the call, and your prevailing fears of its dissolution if I refuse, have given me ground to believe that the voice of this church is the voice of Christ.[7]

"With a great sense of [his] own inability," Watts agreed to become the pastor of Mark Lane Chapel, "so far as God shall enlighten and strengthen me." On March 29, 1702, as preparation for the Lord's Supper, Watts preached a sermon on 1 Corinthians 10:17, "wherein he showed how much our communion with each other as well as with Christ was set forth and sealed in this great ordinance," that it might serve "as a new covenant with the Lord and with each other also." The record

book of the chapel then records that after the supper they sang
"a gospel hymn suitable to the ordinance taken from Revelation 1:5–7."[8] Watts had written the hymn for this occasion.

Now to the Lord, that makes us know
The wonders of his dying love,
Be humble honors paid below,
And strains of nobler praise above. . . .

To Jesus our atoning Priest,
To Jesus our superior King,
Be everlasting power confess'd,
And every tongue his glory sing.[9]

The clerk of the chapel recorded that the congregation sang "with one heart and one voice, the glory of our
Redeemer and our great consolation and joy."[10] Two things
are particularly notable: the biblical text for this hymn is not
taken from the Psalms, and there was apparently no public
outcry against their pastor's violating the strictures of exclusive
psalmody; the outcry would come in many places, but not
here at Mark Lane Chapel. Watts had winsomely begun the
"Watts revolution" in Christian worship, and his people loved
it. Watts' warm preaching was noteworthy for its "depth of
preparation and resulting maturity of teaching," and in that
preparation Watts began a pattern of crafting a hymn that
adorned the central message of the text he was expounding

in the sermon. Week by week his congregation drank deeply at the well of those sermons and had its spiritual imagination awakened in the accompanying hymn. The dwindling attendance reversed, and within a short time more than 500 people gathered at Mark Lane to hear the young man preach—and to sing his hymns. Eventually the growing congregation was forced to move to a larger meeting house on Bury Street.[11]

SHEPHERD PREACHER

Samuel Johnson observed that Nonconformist preachers had previously been suspicious of eloquence and had "obscured and blunted" their delivery, in his opinion, "by coarseness and inelegance of style." But Watts, according to Johnson, "showed them that zeal and purity might be expressed and enforced by polished diction." Eminent in the literary world in Watts' own day, Johnson gives us a contemporary lens into Watts as a preacher and pastor. "In the pulpit, though his low stature, which very little exceeded five feet, graced him with no advantages of appearance, yet the gravity and propriety of his utterance made his discourses very efficacious." Johnson compared the physically unimpressive Watts to one of the foremost orators of London and concluded that Watts was greatly the superior in the "art of pronunciation."[12]

Five feet tall? Imagine the vertically challenged Watts, a grown man the height of my eldest daughter, stepping into the pulpit to proclaim the gospel to his flock. Mark Lane Chapel had grown used to giants in that pulpit, but the congregation wisely did not measure Watts' worth by his stature.

A story is told that reveals both how popular Watts had become in London and how diminutive he was in stature. A man seeing Watts for the first time at a London coffeehouse expressed astonishment and scorn at Watts' unimpressive appearance. "Is that the great Dr. Watts?" he asked. Watts, overhearing, replied with a quatrain from his *Horae Lyricae*:

> *Were I so tall to reach the pole,*
> *Or grasp the ocean with my span,*
> *I must be measur'd by my soul:*
> *The mind's the standard of the man.*[13]

In keeping with his unimposing stature, he lacked a deep, commanding preacher's voice that could echo through the rafters and shake the windows. His voice was described as thin and gentle, not unappealing but without force in itself. Watts had to rely on depth, substance, imagination, and sanctified eloquence rather than brute force in his delivery. He did not make much use of hand movements as he spoke; Johnson wrote, "He did not endeavor to assist his eloquence by any gesticulations." But Watts, who was a keen observer of those around him, especially of his congregation, and who understood as a poet that "wait makes weight," made the best use of the short pause in his delivery: "At the conclusion of weighty sentences he gave time, by a short pause, for the proper impression."[14]

Knowing his own need of grace and strength, Watts never went into the pulpit without much prayer. He had learned to pray from his godly father, who taught him as a child "to beg God to help you to pray." His father tenderly instructed him in praying, "though it may want form of words, yet if the heart be in it, this is prayer, and such prayer too as God will hear and accept." In public praying with his congregation, Watts had, as his father called them, "praying gifts and praying graces," and was described as "remarkably distinct, perspicuous, and solemn."[15] Watts himself described praying as a "conversation with God above while we are here below." Upon taking up his duties as pastor of Mark Lane, Watts resided near the chapel with the family of Thomas Hollis. There, Watts set aside a "secret chamber" for private prayer, where he regularly called on his great God to animate his preaching and his poetry. "Abandon the secret chamber," wrote Watts, "and the spiritual life will decay."[16] He also knew that it was impossible for him to preach and guide his flock if his own spiritual life was lacking conversation with God.

Early in his preaching ministry, Watts wrote out each sermon in manuscript, but he was careful not to confine himself too closely to his prepared text, "amplifying and altering as he found inclination or occasion, and that with the utmost freedom." Johnson describes Watts as he gained maturity as a preacher: "Such was his flow of thoughts, and such his promptitude of language, that in the latter part of his life he did not precompose his cursory sermons, but, having adjusted the heads and sketched out some particulars, trusted for success to his extemporary powers."[17] Perhaps Watts found that by carefully studying the biblical text and by organizing its meaning in poetic verse in a hymn, the meaning of the text became so rooted in his understanding that he no longer needed to rely on a written sermon manuscript.

Watts' physical weakness disadvantaged him in his role as a pastor. So loved was he by his congregation in the pulpit that they longed for pastoral visits in their homes. Watts attempted to both preach and make regular pastoral visits:

> To stated and public instruction he added familiar visits and personal application, and was careful to improve the opportunities which conversation offered of diffusing and increasing the influence of religion. By his natural temper he was quick of resentment; but by his established and habitual practice he was gentle, modest, and inoffensive. His tenderness appeared in his attention to children, and to the poor.[18]

But his fragile health would not allow him to sustain the frequent visits that he desired to make to the homes of his congregants. Due to the limitations of his health, in July 1703, the now much larger congregation provided Watts with an assistant, Samuel Price, with whom Watts served in friendship and mutual respect for the remainder of his ministry.[19]

These years of preparing sermons required Watts to dig

deeply into the meaning of the inspired text. Preaching forced him to copiously cross-reference biblical themes, to compare Scripture with Scripture, to take deeply into his soul the sacred history, figurative language, imaginative comparisons, and doctrinal truths of the Bible. And he had to stand before his congregation, made up of rich and poor, high-born and common, elderly, middle-aged, newly married, and teenage, and even children and lisping toddlers. Few things could have prepared him to awaken the imagination of his hearers better than these years of close, precise biblical study and exposition.

Watts' hymns, not surprisingly, have been called rhymed sermons.[20] Because they were undiluted theology conveyed to the mind and heart through Watts' poetic imagination and gifted wonder, his people—and all who sing Watts' hymns today—were dazzled with the splendor of Christ and the gospel. Through his hymns, his flock apprehended biblical truth with both mind and spirit. Watts' theology became their theology; his doxology became their doxology.

WATTS: GOSPEL FAITHFULNESS IN WEAKNESS

Whatever weakness and inadequacy Watts encountered, he found grace to help in time of need. Whether it was being vertically challenged or dealing with chronic illness and pain, Watts kept his eyes on what was most important. Gifted as he was, he cared nothing about being known as a great poet; he wanted his life to be a reflection of the grace of the gospel. He was determined to use his gifts to make known to others the glories of the Savior and the forgiveness of sins that was to be had in Christ alone.

Your calling and mine are very different from that of a man of Watts' genius. There is no mistake about that for most of us. Who of us, however, has not felt the weakness and inadequacy that Watts daily felt? Yet, he was enabled by grace to persist in gospel faithfulness through it all. And he has left us his sermon hymns, composed while he endured pounding headaches and while he attempted to navigate his role as a subordinate to a minister he knew was not an effective preacher.

Watts models how a Christian lives and serves in a less-than-perfect world. He demonstrates how ordinary Christians are to seek the Lord in earnest prayer, and thereby find hope in the afflictions and bewilderments of life in a broken world, one that is gloriously seasoned by the grace and beauty of the gospel of Jesus Christ.

CHAPTER FOUR

Watts as Lyric Poet

Through his acquaintance with influential Nonconformists in London, Isaac Watts had met Sir Thomas Abney, who had a palatial house at Highgate Hill, London, and another, Abney House, in fashionable Newington, where Watts had studied. The Abneys and Watts forged an immediate friendship, and Abney, who was lord mayor of London, appointed Watts to be his chaplain.

Though he had thrown in his lot with Nonconformity, Abney was required, as lord mayor, to occasionally conform to Anglicanism by taking Communion at an established church. Just as he had great respect for his Anglican schoolmaster, the Rev. John Pinhorne, so Watts seems to have had no difficulty with Abney's occasional conformity to Anglican Communion. Watts always attempted to find the greatest unity possible between those with whom he differed, as seen in his later proposal to unite the Congregationalists and Baptists by offering to give up the doctrine of infant baptism if his Baptist brethren would give up immersion. They would not. (It is possible Watts had foreseen the outcome and so was taking less theological risk with the proposal than it may seem.)

Unfortunately, other Nonconformists were not so tolerant of Abney's practice. They published pamphlets critical of his double-mindedness and suggested that Abney should remain at his home singing "Psalms at Highgate Hill" and "splitting texts with his diminutive figure of a chaplain." Daniel Defoe, the author of *Robinson Crusoe*, joined in and called Abney's conformity "a-playing at bo-peep with God Almighty."[1]

During this time, Watts suffered almost continually from a disorder of the stomach and from frequent pains in the head. He tried many cures, including going to Bath and Tunbridge, and making visits home to the countryside in Southampton. Hoping that fresh air and exercise would help, he even purchased a horse which he rode more than eight hundred miles in five months. There were brief seasons of some degree of relief, but never a cure. Always the disorder returned, and when it did, Watts found preaching difficult.[2]

During one of Watts' bouts with illness, he was invited to come to Abney Park to regain his health. Abney Park was one of the finest estates of the wealthy Puritans in London. It had an ancient castlelike structure, a newer house built with brick in the Neoclassical style, and vast lawns and neatly trimmed gardens surrounded by yew and cedar trees. Watts intended to stay for two weeks, but he remained—at the insistence of his host—for the better part of thirty-six years. He continued to ride into the city and preach to his congregation when he was able, but he always came back to Abney Park to rest and to write.

Here, amid the manicured grounds, the ornamental pools, the bird sanctuary, and the prominent hillock, Watts found inspiration for his writing, especially for his poetry. Due to his habit of climbing the hillock, gazing out over the estate, and writing, it was later named Watts Mount.[3]

First Published Poems

In 1705, at the encouragement of his brother Enoch and others, Watts published his first collection of poems, *Horae Lyricae*, or *Lyrical Hours*. The volume was divided into three books: the first contained poems for devotion and piety; the second, poems about virtue, honor, and friendship; and the third, poems to the memory of the dead.[4] In his preface, Watts made clear that, though some might consider the work to be secular poetry, he intended nothing in the volume to be dishonoring to God: "Among the songs that are dedicated to divine love, I think I may be bold to assert, that I never composed one line of them with any other design than that they are applied to here; I have endeavored to secure them all from being perverted and debased to wanton pleasure."[5]

Thus, giving his apology in prose, Watts in verse proceeded to denounce the "fabled muse's art" and claim heartfelt genuineness for his poetry:

Regard the man, who, in seraphic lays,
And flowing numbers, sings his Maker's praise:
He needs invoke no fabled muse's art,
The heav'nly song comes genuine from his heart.[6]

In a society that arguably valued literary genius above the other arts, *Horae Lyricae* established Watts in literary circles as a poet of the first rank. However, there are critics who argue that Watts was a far better poet when writing hymns and that he showed evidence of some of the literary "vices" of the age in *Horae Lyricae*. He has been chided for "forsaking simplicity and nature, and following artificial models and straining after affected diction,"[7] all things he seldom did in his hymns.

SMITTEN WITH AN ADMIRER

As happens with popular authors' works, Watts' *Horae Lyricae* began drawing fan mail. One such letter came from a young woman, Elizabeth Singer, a poetess in her own right. Her father was a friend of Thomas Ken, author of the Morning, Evening, and Midnight hymns, all three ending with the well-known doxology "Praise God from whom all blessings flow." Ken had encouraged Elizabeth's poetic interests and had urged her to begin a versification of Job 38.[8]

Elizabeth wrote Watts a versified fan letter in which she, perhaps a bit indiscreetly, said that his poetry on love made her forget all her other suitors and gave her a deep desire to meet him. When they met, Watts, who had thought himself above susceptibility to romantic love, was smitten. Standing before him was a lovely woman with shining auburn hair, sparkling blue eyes, and a fair complexion with, as Watts described her, a "lovely blush" on her cheeks. Her carriage was gracious and her voice was "harmoniously sweet." She was just Watts' age and, what is more, she wasn't too tall. What she saw was another matter: "Before her stood not even a moderately presentable Englishman, but a minute, sallow-faced anatomy with hook nose, prominent cheekbones, heavy countenance, pale complexion, and small gray eyes."[9]

Watts, however, was not about to let the opportunity pass him by. This man of eloquence, the celebrated poet of *Horae Lyricae*, had given hints of his longings "for social bliss," that is, for marriage:

Give me a blessing fit to match my mind,
A kindred soul to double and to share my joys.[10]

He was sure the lovely woman before him must be the fulfillment of those longings. Therefore, he formulated his words and made ready to propose marriage to her. But when he did so, Elizabeth gently but candidly declined. "Mr. Watts," she said, "I only wish I could say that I admire the casket as much as I admire the jewel."[11] She could not see herself married to a man whose jewel, whose inner poetic beauty, was encased in such an unattractive shell.

Watts may have inadvertently expressed some of his for-givable disappointment at being slighted by Miss Singer in a hymn entitled "Love to the Creatures Dangerous," as seen in these representative stanzas:

> *How vain are all things here below!*
> *How false, and yet how fair!*
> *Each pleasure hath its poison too,*
> *And every sweet a snare.*
>
> *The brightest things below the sky*
> *Give but a flattering light;*
> *We should suspect some danger nigh*
> *Where we possess delight.*
>
> *The fondness of a creature's love,*
> *How strong it strikes the sense!*
> *Thither the warm affections move,*
> *Nor can we call them thence.*[12]

We feel in these lines how deeply Watts' own senses had been stricken by Elizabeth and how difficult it must have been for him to call his romantic affections away from her beauty. Watts and Miss Singer, however, managed to remain friends from afar and kept up an active correspondence throughout their lives. At thirty-five, she married the nephew (who was twenty-two) of Watts' instructor Thomas Rowe[13]; Watts never married. He concluded his jilted love poem in keeping with his Christ-centered outlook on all of his life:

Dear Savior, let thy beauties be
My soul's eternal food.[14]

His next published collection of poems would even more clearly keep the beauties of his dear Savior before his and his readers' minds and hearts.

WATTS: USING GIFTS
FOR THE HIGHEST PURPOSE

As a lyric poet, Watts was no doubt tempted to reorganize his priorities and clamor after the adulation of the literary world with his pen. But this episode in his life demonstrates that grace prevailed, and so he persisted in keeping his eyes on Jesus as he used his gifts.

Watts' determination to do everything to the glory of God, even writing lyric poetry not specifically intended for singing the praises of God, can help the vast majority of Christians who work daily at secular callings. Whether you are a farmer or a CEO, a construction worker or an academic, a mother or a managing editor, you, like Watts, want your work to bring honor to the name of Christ.

Moreover, as Watts experienced, who among us has not had disappointments of one kind or another? In some instances, they may be minor setbacks; in others, as it was for Watts, they may be disappointments that profoundly alter our hopes and dreams for the rest of our lives. Smitten with love for a woman he would never be able to marry, Watts pressed on, believing that God had ordained good for his life, regardless of the disappointment and loneliness through which he was passing.

So it is for each of us. As with Watts, we see only dimly through the bewildering mysteries of life. Yet as Watts did, by grace alone, we too can know and believe that God has portioned out our lives for His glory and for our good. And strong in faith, upheld by divine love, we, too, can see through the gloom and sing the praises of our Savior, who passed through far deeper woes than ever Watts or we will endure.

CHAPTER FIVE

Watts as Hymn Writer

Renowned hymnologist Erik Routley said of Isaac Watts, "Of all our hymn writers he scaled the greatest heights and plumbed the most bathetic abysses."[1] Though Bernard L. Manning considered Charles Wesley a greater poetic artist, he said Watts' poetry "is pure and transparent," and compared the "magical quality in his verse" to that of John Milton and Dante Alighieri. He singularly credits Watts with giving singing back to the English-speaking congregation: "All later hymn writers, even those who excel [Watts], are his debtors."[2] There are many reasons for this, but one clear one is that Watts began working on his craft at an early age.

By 1707, Watts' thirty-third year, he had been writing hymns for more than half of his life. From his first effort as a teen to the more mature biblical and expository hymns of his pastoral ministry at Mark Lane Chapel, Watts had written 210 hymns along with twelve short doxologies. His first edition of *Hymns and Spiritual Songs* (1707) was enthusiastically received by Nonconformist congregations, first in England, but soon far afield in the American Colonies. Watts expanded his hymn collection in 1709 to include 345 hymns and fifteen short doxologies. Significantly, one of the doxologies was to be sung in praise of the Trinity; it included lines seemingly resolving Watts' intellectual struggles with God's triune nature:

Where reason fails
With all her powers,
There faith prevails
And love adores.[3]

Watts eventually would write some seven hundred hymns, of which most hymnals include only twenty or thirty. To be blunt, many of his hymns are gawky and crude. But Wesley wrote six thousand hymns, and we sing still fewer of his than Watts'. Watts was the pioneer; he was launching into uncharted poetic and liturgical depths. As one critic has put it: "We must expect him to make many experiments that fail, and to try many arrangements before he finds the best. Only in a few places can we expect him to bring one off."[4]

Watts labored under several disadvantages, some self-imposed, others imposed upon him. He was a literary genius, but he nevertheless confined himself consciously to writing poetry for everyone to sing in the worship of God—children, the poor, the uneducated, and those with no musical training. He confined himself to writing in only a few simple meters that had existing tunes that were familiar to congregations. Moreover, he always tried to make his poetry workable in the "lining out" method of singing, in which the leader sang out a line and the congregation repeated it after him, and so forth throughout the hymn.[5] Critics who fail to take these restrictions into account disqualify their opinions about Watts and are unhelpful in forming ours.

Christians have been both praised and vilified for their singing. While yet an unbeliever, Augustine wept when he heard Christians singing hymns, "touched to the very quick by the notes of the Church so sweetly singing."[6] On the other hand, in a letter dated December 7, 1950, C. S. Lewis wrote, "I naturally loathe nearly all hymns; the face and the life of the charwoman in the next pew who revels in them, teach me that good taste in poetry or music are not necessary to salvation."[7] Known for his generosity toward others, Lewis' thinly veiled conceit embarrasses us. But God was not finished with Lewis. In "Answers to Questions on Christianity," one of the essays in his book *God in the Dock*, Lewis reflected on becoming a Christian and thinking he was above needing to go to church and sing hymns: "I disliked very much their hymns, which I considered to be fifth-rate poems set to sixth-rate music." As he fellowshipped with Christians of all walks of life, however, this "conceit just began peeling off. I realized that the hymns (which were just sixth-rate music) were, nevertheless, being sung with devotion and benefit by an old saint in elastic-side boots in the opposite pew, and then you realize that you aren't fit to clean those boots. It gets you out of your solitary conceit."[8]

It would seem that in these reflections Lewis comes, if not full circle, at least to a dramatically improved understanding of Christians and of Christian worship. His former view may have had something to do with the destructive effect both modernism and postmodernism were exerting on rating the worth of poetry—after all, Lewis must own up as author of these lines:

Ho, rumble, rumble, rumble,
Rumble drum belaboured.[9]

I wouldn't care to attempt rating that as poetry on any scale.

Moreover, it is generally agreed that everything Lewis wrote about in poetry, he wrote far more effectively about elsewhere in his prose. But the real hurdle for Lewis with regard to hymns may have had much more to do with him developing both a deeper love for his neighbor and for Christ, the object of the hymns he so disliked.

Whether Lewis was referring to Watts in any of these reflections is unknown. At Holy Trinity, the parish church in Headington Quarry that Lewis attended, he would have sung from *Hymns Ancient and Modern*, the authorized Anglican hymnal, which included many Watts hymns. There is a great deal in Watts that could have helped unmask Lewis' self-conceit and turn his face toward Christ and his neighbor.

The scope of this work will not allow an examination of all of the best from Watts' canon of hymns, but along with his "When I Survey the Wondrous Cross" and others already featured, this chapter will consider several of the hymns that compelled later generations to acknowledge their profound debt to Watts and call him "the Father of English Hymnody."

"ALAS! AND DID MY SAVIOR BLEED"

The following hymn begs comparison with Watts' arguably best-loved hymn, "When I Survey the Wondrous Cross." Here, however, he employs a series of rhetorical questions in his first two stanzas, which draw the worshiper into a first-person point of view. This makes genuine to the individual soul the stupendous reality of the "crimes that I have done," for which the Savior "devot[ed] that sacred head" and bled and died for "such a worm as I":

Alas! and did my Savior bleed?
And did my Sovereign die?
Would he devote that sacred head,
For such a worm as I?

Was it for crimes that I have done
He groaned upon the tree?

Amazing pity! Grace unknown!
And love beyond degree![10]

Watts' wonder is invoked in the final two lines of the quatrain above. The poet, and hence, the worshiper, is caught up in the wonder of Christ's pity, grace, and love so incalculably beyond human knowing.

Next, Watts shifts to an interpretation of a historical moment in the crucifixion: when somber darkness descended over the scene at Calvary for three hours. Watts awakens our spiritual understanding with his imaginative explanation for the reasonableness of that darkness given the cosmic circumstances that caused it to descend:

Well might the sun in darkness hide,
And shut his glories in,
When Christ the mighty Maker died
For man the creature's sin.

Just as the sun was compelled to hide its face at the stupendous scene unfolding, so the persona in Watts' poem is compelled to hide his face in shame "While [Christ's] dear cross appears":

Thus might I hide my blushing face
While his dear cross appears,

Dissolve my heart in thankfulness,
And melt mine eyes in tears.

One of the endearing qualities of Watts' poetry is his preference for simple language over the ornate, as employed here and in his best hymns. But that does not mean he uses flabby or pedestrian verbiage. Watts summons up vigorous verbs, an essential key to any good writing, poetry or prose. His choice of the word *dissolve* powerfully suggests the immeasurable extent of the gratitude owed to the Savior for such "love beyond degree."

Then, as Watts is so careful to do in many of his hymns, he draws the singer and worshiper into a resolution of abandonment and a radical, heartfelt consecration.

But drops of grief can ne'er repay
The debt of love I owe;
Here, Lord, I give myself away
'Tis all that I can do.

One cannot help but hear similarities in the consecration of the final stanza of "When I Survey":

Were the whole realm of nature mine,
That were a present far too small;
Love so amazing, so divine,
Demands my soul, my life, my all.[11]

Even if our hearts were to be dissolved and our eyes melted with tears of grief, it would in no way be proportionate to the "debt of love" we owe for "Love so amazing, so divine." Watts knew there was no work of righteousness we could do to earn such divine love. This was grace alone accomplished at infinite cost by Christ alone, plus nothing. We cannot begin to repay the Savior's love with tears or, even if it were possible, to give Him the "whole realm of nature" as a present. Such "love beyond degree" invokes deep, heartfelt thankfulness expressed in giving ourselves away; or, to put it another way, "love so amazing . . . demands my soul, my life, my all."

"Martyrdom," the tune most often used for "Alas! and Did My Savior Bleed," was composed by Hugh Wilson in 1800 and arranged by Robert Smith in 1825.[12] It is a solid musical arrangement, though it may not be the very best tune for this text. Serviceable as it is, there is the sense that the rising notes are doing so on their own initiative, without specific warrant or prompting from the meaning of the words in the poetry. This is, alas, not an uncommon problem with hymns and tunes. Nevertheless, "Martyrdom" is better than many tunes and has stood the test of time in its association with this incomparable Watts hymn text.

"JOIN ALL THE GLORIOUS NAMES"

Watts penned the following hymn based on Paul's words to the Philippians, "God has highly exalted him and bestowed on him the name that is above every name" (2:9). One can imagine Watts preparing to preach a sermon on this text to his beloved flock at Mark Lane Chapel. As he studied, his biblically informed imagination would have bolted into action. After preaching the sermon, he would have introduced the hymn, perhaps looking out on the hoary head of John Owen's widow sitting in the front row, or on Oliver Cromwell's son Richard sitting ramrod straight in his seat, hands on his knees.

The congregation would not have sung it to John Darwall's excellent tune that bears his name; it was not written until 1770.[13] But if they had heard "Darwall," I'm convinced that they would have wanted to sing this Watts text to it. The tune rises with energy, ascending appropriately as Watts explores the biblical names for God: Wisdom, Love, Power, Prophet, High Priest, Counselor, Savior, Lord, Conqueror, and King. So perfectly does "Darwall" adorn the text that the composer must have had this poem of Watts' sitting before him on his desk as he wrote the music. The melody might be difficult for people with less musical experience to sing at first, but once they hear it they gain the sense that the tune is wedded almost perfectly to the poetry, and when they see everyone around them drawn with delight to the meaning of the words by the escalating energy in the final two bars, learning the tune seems very much worth the effort:

Join all the glorious names
Of wisdom, love, and pow'r,

That ever mortals knew,
That angels ever bore:
All are too poor to speak his worth,
Too poor to set my Savior forth.

Great Prophet of my God,
My tongue would bless thy name:
By thee the joyful news
Of our salvation came;
The joyful news of sins forgiv'n,
Of hell subdued and peace with heaven.

Thou art my Counselor,
My pattern and my Guide,
And thou my Shepherd art,
O keep me near thy side;
Nor let my feet e'er turn astray
To wander in the crooked way.

We love the Shepherd's voice;
His watchful eye shall keep
Our pilgrim souls among
The thousands of God's sheep;
He feeds his flock, he calls their names,
And gently leads the tender lambs.[14]

OTHER WATTS FAVORITES

Though it has not ranked as highly as other Watts hymns, the following first stanza of the hymn "Give Me the Wings of Faith to Rise" perfectly illustrates what makes Watts such an able hymn writer:

> *Give me the wings of faith to rise*
> *within the veil, and see*
> *the saints above, how great their joys,*
> *how bright their glories be.*[15]

In the best of his hymns, Watts does precisely that: he opens the eyes of our faith, gives wings to our imagination, pulls back the veil, and shows us the bright glories of Christ and the gospel—sometimes in graphic ways.

There is an odd story connected to Watts' hymn "Not All the Blood of Beasts," which begins with the quatrain:

> *Not all the blood of beasts*
> *On Jewish altars slain*
> *Could give the guilty conscience peace,*
> *Or wash away its stain.*[16]

The story may be conjecture, but it has been told that Watts found inspiration for this hymn while walking through the market in Smithfield, London. Surrounded by the newly slaughtered beasts on display for sale in the market, Watts may have taken refuge in a coffeehouse and penned the opening lines.[17] More likely the real inspiration, as always seems to be the case with Watts, is a biblical one: "It is impossible for the blood of bulls and goats to take away sins" (Heb. 10:4). So Watts extols the "redeeming love" of "Christ, the heavenly Lamb," who alone takes all His people's sins away with His far richer blood.

During the Great Awakening, Watts' hymns played a central role. George Whitefield used Watts' hymns in his outdoor preaching throughout Georgia and New England. Likewise, Watts' hymns had a significant impact on African slaves in the American Colonies. Presbyterian preacher Samuel Davies, an itinerant evangelist and pastor in Anglican Virginia, asked wealthy supporters to donate books to enable his efforts to teach slaves to read. They contributed many volumes of Watts' *Hymns and Spiritual Songs*, which Davies gave to slaves who were members of his congregations. Davies described how his kitchen would be full late into the night with slaves who had gathered there to sing Watts.[18] The simplicity and sensual passion of Watts' poetry transcended racial and ethnic barriers, and the recurring theme of the suffering of the Savior for lost sinners was a message that resonated with the oppression of African slaves. Also, Watts' determination to avoid flowery, multisyllabic language made his hymns accessible to people who were not yet literate, and the simple metrical structure lent itself to the call-and-response singing of African worship. It is not difficult to imagine these lines from Watts being sung in this manner:

> *When I can read my title clear*
> *To mansions in the skies,*
> *I bid farewell to every fear,*
> *And wipe my weeping eyes.*[19]

One theory says that the spirituals created by anonymous African slaves over the next 150 years got their name from Watts' title, *Hymns and Spiritual Songs*.

WATTS: NOT OF AN AGE BUT FOR ALL TIME

Watts' hymns are, in fact, for every Christian in every age— perhaps especially for those in times engaged in a perpetual war with permanence, like ours. If it may be said, "All later hymn writers, even those who excel [Watts], are his debtors,"[20] it may equally be deduced that those who ignore Watts will never excel him. And such neglect will be to the enduring detriment of both theological substance and genuine heartfelt passion in the worship of God.

With Watts, it is not only the poet who is caught up in the wonder of Christ's pity, grace, and love so far beyond human knowing but also we, through his poetic appeal to our senses, have our imaginations awakened to the deepest and the highest things of God. Watts gives the worshiper words to sing that are worthy of the grand object of sung praise. In our slavishly narcissistic age, a recovery of Watts will help turn us from ourselves to the God who alone redeems sinners and is alone supremely worthy of our praises. Watts is able to do this not only because of the brilliance of his poetry, but because of the way he employs the poetry to adorn the beauty of Christian theology.

CHAPTER SIX

Watts as Poet Theologian

Hymnologists seem to agree that "Watts' hymns are rhymed theology."[1] As a preacher and poet, Watts preached doctrinal sermons and also wrote hymns that gave his congregation poetically adorned instruction in important biblical doctrines.

How did Watts marry theology and poetry? We can answer by examining some of the major doctrines of his poetry and analyzing one of his most theological hymns.

THE TRINITY

There were times in his ministry when Watts was confused about the doctrine of the Trinity. He has even been accused by critics of being an Arian, one who, like Arius

(c. AD 250–336) of old, denied the Trinity. Surrounded by Enlightenment rationalism, Watts was forced to grapple with intellectual arguments against the orthodox view that God could be both one and three. Furthermore, among all his other achievements, Watts was something of a mathematician.[2] The Trinity was a doctrine that seemed to require him to suspend his rational mathematical knowledge. In orthodox Christian theology, one plus one plus one equals both three and one.

But Watts drew from the godly instruction of his father in dealing with this doctrine. He recognized that his doubts needed to be informed by God's Word, not man's word. Therefore, he developed a method of taming his reason when it seemed to conflict with the Bible. Observe the importance for Watts of interpreting Scripture by "the analogy of faith," that is, by comparing Scripture with Scripture:

> In matters of the Christian faith, I would make the Scriptures my guide. . . . My reason should be used as a necessary instrument to compare the several parts of revelation together, to discover their mutual explication, as well as to judge whether they run counter to any dictates of natural light. But, if an inquisitive mind over-leap the bounds of faith, and give the reins to all our reasonings upon divine themes in so wide and open a field as that of possibles and probables, it is no easy matter to guess where they will stop their career.[3]

The philosophical air Watts breathed was that of the Enlightenment, which R. C. Sproul has aptly termed "The Endarkenment," and the Age of Reason encouraged many a young man to "over-leap the bounds of faith," as Watts put it in the quotation above. It is no surprise, then, that a man of Watts' intellect, living in a world of the mind, was forced seriously to grapple with the apparent paradoxes posed by human reason and faith. What is refreshing is that Watts did not in the end over-leap the bounds of orthodox Christianity. He explained the method by which he reined in his human reason by Holy Scripture:

> When I have given my thoughts a loose, and let them rove without confinement, sometimes I seem to have carried reason with me even to the camp of Socinus; but then St. John gives my soul a twitch, and St. Paul bears me back again (if I mistake not his meaning) almost to the tents of Calvin.[4]

Socinus was the sixteenth-century Polish founder of an anti-Trinitarian intellectual movement, and for a time Watts found his reason drawn to Socinian conclusions. But then he received, as he quaintly put it, a "twitch" from the Gospels or the Apostle Paul, and was brought back into the orthodox Calvinist theology of the Trinity.

Critics of Watts like to make his period of confusion about the nature of the Trinity the sum total of who he was. But

Watts' treatise *The Gift of the Spirit* makes clear the orthodoxy of his theological understanding. In it, he wrote, in something akin to an ecstasy, "How the wondrous doctrine of the blessed Trinity shines through the whole of our religion, and sheds a glory upon every part of it!" He added:

> What is dearer to God the Father than his only Son? And what diviner blessing has He to bestow upon men than his Holy Spirit? Yet has He given his Son for us; and by the hands of his Son He confers his blessed Spirit on us: "Jesus having received of the Father the promise of the Spirit, shed it forth on men" (Acts 2:33).[5]

As a young scholar, Watts worked the meaning of the books he was reading—whether Socinus, Aristotle, or Calvin—into his memory by both abridgment and amplification, always comparing and tempering his conclusions with Holy Scripture.

At one such time, Watts explored the validity of the idea that the Holy Spirit was not a separate personality in the Godhead, but more of a figure of speech for the spirit of God at work in providence and the salvation of sinners. It is even claimed that Watts argued against praying to the Holy Spirit. But when the theoretical must give way to the doxological, as is the case in the writing of a hymn, doxology can help stabilize theology. It is very difficult to sing bad theology. Knowing that what one is putting down with the pen will be taken up on the lips of worshipers acts as a corrective to flawed theology. When writing a hymn, men such as Watts can be at their theological best. In the following hymn quatrain, Watts is specifically praying to and worshiping the Holy Spirit:

Come Holy Spirit, heav'nly Dove,
With all your quick'ning pow'rs;
Kindle a flame of sacred love,
In these cold hearts of ours.[6]

It is difficult to imagine such a quatrain written by a poet who did not believe the Holy Spirit was a co-equal member of the Trinity and, as such, a worthy object to address in both prayer and worship.

In the concluding stanza of the hymn, Watts repeated the first two lines and ended by petitioning the Holy Spirit to give the Savior's love as a means of animating our own love and worship:

Come, shed abroad a Savior's love,
And that shall kindle ours.[7]

GOD'S CREATION

"Watts is Milton's disciple," hymnologist Bernard L. Manning wrote, drawing specific attention to how often John Milton wrote about the sky. This similarity between Watts and Milton is not surprising given Watts' love of the natural world and his determination to see the Creator's hand and care in every detail. It has been said of Watts, he saw "the world in a grain of sand and eternity in an hour."[8] His imagination was transfixed by the vast expanse of the firmament, and this fascination served as a means to extol redemption in Christ, the Word:

> *Ere the blue heavens were stretched abroad*
> *From everlasting was the Word.*[9]

As Samuel Johnson concluded, Watts' every motive for writing was made "subservient to evangelical instruction."[10] Hence, Watts' hymns are the product of his motive to adorn instruction with "words set in delightful proportion,"[11] as Sir Philip Sidney defined poetry.

DIVINE SOVEREIGNTY

As a biblically informed theologian and preacher, Watts found his mind and imagination drawn to meditation on the infinity of the God who, by His power and authority, laid out and sustained the heavens and the entire universe. Describing Watts' fascination with the immensity of the sky and heavens, Manning wrote, "In Watts it leads straight to the Calvinist's awareness of the sovereignty of God."[12] Watts winsomely wove this awareness of God's sovereignty in all areas—including salvation—throughout his hymns, as summarized here in a quatrain:

The sovereign will of God alone
Creates us heirs of grace,
Born in the image of His Son,
A new, peculiar race.[13]

Watts spoke of God's sovereignty when he wrote of his plans to introduce new poetry into the sung worship of the church: "Leave a man, leave a church free to worship and to wonder at the almighty power and grace of God." Commenting on this, Erik Routley wrote that Watts "was [a] Calvinist. The quality which is common to all Watts' work, is this wonder, which is the essence of John Calvin's message."[14]

Hymnologist Albert Bailey reluctantly admitted, "Watts' hymns are rhymed theology, and the theology is derived from John Calvin, who in turn got his basic ideas from Augustine and Paul." Bailey, a theological liberal, despised the Calvinism of Nonconformists, Puritans, and Presbyterians: "This religion is nothing short of dreadful. It outrages our sense of justice, contradicts our reason, makes God a monster, Christ a play-actor in the tragedy of human history, and robs man of his freedom without which a moral life is impossible."[15] Hence, it is no surprise that Bailey was bewildered by lines like these:

May not the sovereign Lord on high
Dispense his favors as he will;
Choose some to life while others die,
And yet be just and gracious still?[16]

Bailey's answer was that God could *not* choose some to salvation and be just and gracious still. Yet he seemed, nevertheless, to have been enamored with Watts as a hymn writer, and went so far as to claim that Watts "admirably" fulfills Milton's description of the finest poetry as "simple, sensual, and passionate." At last, theological skeptic that he was, Bailey was forced to conclude that with Watts, "Even the cold logic of Calvinism catches fire."[17]

For Watts, there was no "cold logic" to Calvinism. Calvinism was merely the theological name that had attached itself to the biblical truths that filled Watts with wonder, love, and gratitude at the immensity of free grace set upon unworthy sinners before the foundation of the world and accomplished and applied by Jesus Christ through the transforming power of the Holy Spirit regenerating the hearts of the unworthy elect. Watts believed Calvinism was worth singing about because it was the theological glue that gave glory to the grace of God in Christ for the salvation of sinners.

"WHY WAS I A GUEST?"

So it was that Watts may have been working on a sermon based on Luke 14:16: "A man once gave a great banquet and invited many." Perhaps he had just enjoyed a sumptuous meal as the long-term guest of the Abney family at their estate and, after the meal, had retired for a stroll on Watts' Mount to meditate on his sermon text. As he mused on the biblical image before him, Watts set down a hymn written in preparation for the Lord's Supper, "How Sweet and Awful Is the Place," one of his most winsome Calvinist hymns:

How sweet and awful is the place
With Christ within the doors,
While everlasting love displays
The choicest of her stores!

While all our hearts and all our songs
Join to admire the feast,
Each of us cry with thankful tongues
"Lord, why was I a guest?"[18]

Watts understood that to come and feast with Christ at the Lord's Supper requires a profound awareness of just how unworthy we are. He awakens our spiritual imagination in these lines, and we begin to see ourselves entering into the very presence of Christ Himself, a place that is both awe-inspiring and somehow sweet as well. Laid out before us, "everlasting love" has put on a spread of the richest foods imaginable. In wonder and anticipation, we pull up our chairs at the table.

Watts' poetry is seldom far away from singing, and in the second stanza he has us admiring the feast with songs sung with "thankful tongues," but then asking ourselves with astonishment, "Lord, why was I a guest?" We might be tempted to ask, "What did I do to deserve such rich food and lavish treatment?" But Watts allows us no self-deluded confusion about how we were brought to this place:

"Why was I made to hear Thy voice,
And enter while there's room?
When thousands make a wretched choice
And rather starve than come?"

By means of this rhetorical question, Watts leads us to the only explanation that can make any gospel sense and be in any degree consistent with the grand message of free grace. It is a two-pronged question: First, why was I made to hear and to enter? Second, why do thousands "make a wretched choice / And rather starve than come?" That is, why do thousands not hear and enter, but I did? He answers the question in the next stanza:

'Twas the same love that spread the feast,
That sweetly drew us in,
Else we had still refused to taste,
And perished in our sin.

Watts tells us that we were made, that is, enabled to hear Christ's voice and enabled to enter while there was room. Christ was the "love that spread the feast," and it is, indeed, a sweet place to be, because Christ "sweetly drew us in." Without this sovereign, electing, efficacious love, "we had still refused to taste / And perished in our sin."

With these sublime lines, Watts adorns such rich, Christ-honoring theology that it is hard to imagine the most ardent semi-Pelagian not halting in his theological tracks and falling to his knees. Watts gently hushes those who make the argument that it had to be our free will that made the difference, that it would have been unfair for Christ to have sweetly drawn us in and not everyone else equally, that God makes us robots and Himself a monster if He does not leave the final decision up to us. The Arminian mantra, "God cast a vote, Satan cast a vote, and the sinner casts the deciding vote," sounds pretty hollow next to Watts' poetic adornment of predestination and effectual calling. Watts subtly helps us realize that there is little to sing about if God is not absolutely sovereign over the eternal salvation of sinners. How ridiculous to imagine writing and singing hymns of praise, not of Christ and the sovereign grace of the gospel, but of the free will of sinners for making not a wretched choice but a very clever one.

Then, as if anticipating the "What about evangelism and missions?" objection from critics of his Calvinism, Watts shifts to the universal call of this glorious gospel of free grace, begging God to have pity on the nations and to constrain them to come. Watts' prayer appealing to God to do this is itself an acknowledgment that God must sovereignly accomplish the salvation of the nations, that He must do the work of bringing sinners home:

Pity the nations, O our God,
Constrain the earth to come;

81

Send thy victorious word abroad,
And bring the strangers home.

We long to see thy churches full,
That all the chosen race
May with one voice and heart and soul
Sing thy redeeming grace.

Watts grounds the sung worship of all Christians, throughout time and eternity, not in their choice, but in God's choice, for He has stooped down in pity and love to make undeserving sinners members of "the chosen race."

WATTS: WONDER AT ELECTING LOVE

When I read Watts' hymns, a picture of the poet comes to my mind: a slight, unimpressive figure in an ill-fitting powdered wig, a man falling to his knees, his jaw slack with awe, his eyes gazing heavenward in wonder. There is a childlike enchantment to Watts' poetry, as if it were penned by a man who is discovering the glories of the gospel for the very first time, almost as if he is beside himself with excitement at divine truth, a man intoxicated with the free mercy of God in Christ.

How tragic it is that the very thing the post-conservative church hungers for in its worship is already firmly in place in the sensual richness of Watts' poetry. Penned three hundred years ago, his theologically rich poetic expressions remain intensely relevant to worshipers who love the gospel in every age. Watts truly is for all time.

Who among us has not chafed at the sovereignty of God, His electing love, His particular redemption of unworthy sinners? Who among us does not have friends and loved ones who think that the doctrines of grace make God a monster? Watts provides the perfect and enduring antidote to all our doubts and confusions on this score. Meditate on Watts' hymns, and there will be little wonder that a theological liberal who despised Watts' Calvinism could not help acknowledging that, adorned by Watts' poetry, even "Calvinism catches fire."

CHAPTER SEVEN

Watts as Children's Poet

C. S. Lewis was ridiculed by colleagues at Oxford University for taking seriously his faith in Christ, but he was also an object of contempt by the intellectual elites in his day for writing books for children. It was thought to be beneath the dignity of an Oxford don to stoop to such puerile endeavors. Yet, we find Isaac Watts doing much the same thing, and for the same reasons. Watts no doubt would have agreed with Lewis: "No book is really worth reading at the age of ten which is not equally (and often far more) worth reading at the age of fifty."[1] In Watts, we see the metaphysical scholar pausing in his contemplations to craft poetry for children in the nursery. Samuel Johnson wrote of this dimension of Watts:

> His tenderness appeared in his attention to children, and to the poor. For children he condescended to

lay aside the scholar, the philosopher, and the wit, to write little poems of devotion, and systems of instruction, adapted to their wants and capacities, from the dawn of reason through its gradations of advance in the morning of life. Every man acquainted with the common principles of human action will look with veneration on the writer who is at one time combating Locke, and at another making a catechism for children in their fourth year. A voluntary descent from the dignity of science is perhaps the hardest lesson that humility can teach.[2]

Watts' *Divine Songs Attempted in Easy Language for the Use of Children* (1715) shaped more than two generations of children in England and America. More than one hundred years after Watts' death, Lewis Carroll was convinced that Victorian England was so familiar with Watts' *Divine Songs* that he could include in *Alice in Wonderland* a parody of his poem *Against Idleness and Mischief.* Watts' couplet,

> *How doth the little busy bee*
> *Improve each shining hour?*

became in Carroll's parody,

> *How doth the little crocodile*
> *Improve his shining tail?*[3]

Just as Watts entered diligently into his tutoring duties with the Hartopp children, so he took seriously the instruction of the Abney children while he was an extended-stay guest at Abney House, his residence when writing and publishing his volume of children's poetry. He warmly dedicated *Divine Songs* to the Abney children.[4]

WATTS' PREFACE

In the preface to *Divine Songs*, "To all that are concerned in the Education of Children," Watts warns families and teachers of what "an awful and important charge" they have been entrusted with in the instruction of the children under their care. He warns that "the seeds of misery or happiness in this world, and that to come, are oftentimes sown very early, and therefore whatever may conduce to give the minds of children a relish for virtue and religion" ought to be their primary concern. He next lays out a defense for using poetry in the instruction of children:

Verse was at first designed for the service of God, though it hath been wretchedly abused since. The ancients among the Jews and the Heathens taught their children and disciples the precepts of morality and worship in verse. The children of Israel were commanded to learn the words of the song of Moses, Deuteronomy 31:19, 30. And we are directed in the

New Testament, not only to sing with grace in the heart, but to teach and admonish one another by hymns and songs (Ephesians 5:19).[5]

Then, in classic Puritan fashion, Watts presents multiple advantages of using poetry for the nurture of children: "There is a greater delight in the very learning of truths" in poetry which can be so amusing and entertaining." One hears echoes of his argument in his book *The Improvement of the Mind* when he states, "What is learned in verse is longer retained in memory, and sooner recollected," and may prove to be "an effectual means to keep off some temptation, or to incline to some duty." He next argues that filling their minds with *Divine Songs* will help children avoid "emptiness of mind" as a result of learning "the loose and dangerous sonnets of the age."[6]

Watts wrote most of the children's poetry at the request of a schoolmaster friend who was looking for a more effective method of catechizing children in biblical knowledge. Watts assures his readers in the preface that all that followed would be appropriate for "children of all kinds," whether Anglican or Nonconformist; he says that children, "baptized in infancy or not, may all join together in these songs." He explains that he "endeavored to sink the language to the level of a child's understanding, and yet keep it above contempt," hoping thereby that *Divine Songs* would be of "universal use and service," as they, in fact, proved to be for nearly 150 years. He sent this volume forth, asking for a divine benediction on all who were engaged in the "important work of education," and sought God's "abundant graces" so that children who learned his *Divine Songs* might be "a glory amongst the nations" and a "blessing to the earth."[7]

Watts suggested that parents and teachers have their children learn "one of these songs every week," and that when they had ten or twenty of them committed to memory, that they be given their own copies of *Divine Songs*.[8] This was more than a marketing ploy; Watts believed that what he was writing would be an effective means of spiritual nurture for all children—and all the more so if they owned their own copies.

PRAISE TO THE "HEAVENLY KING"

The opening song is a hymn of praise to God that draws a contrast between the smallness of a child and the "dreadful majesty" of "our heav'nly King who reigns above the sky":

> *How glorious is our heav'nly King,*
> *Who reigns above the sky!*
> *How shall a child presume to sing*
> *His dreadful majesty?[9]*

Watts then moves to a poetic adornment of God's power and grace extending beyond the limits of our imagination. He shifts in the fourth stanza to the point of view of a child, one who longs to sing the praises of God with all the saints and angels:

Then let me join this holy train,
And my first offerings bring;
Th' eternal God will not disdain
To hear an infant sing.

It might be argued that in Watts' effort "to sink the language to the level of a child's understanding," he sank into condescension and sentimentality, that he failed to "keep it above contempt." In places, this is certainly the case. Consider, however, that Michelangelo set his hammer and chisel to many a chunk of marble and produced eminently forgettable sculptures before he achieved the triumph of his *David* or the *Pieta*. Watts cannot be fairly criticized for his lesser verses unless the same gauge is used on other great artists. Just as with his hymns, many of his songs for children seem a bit trivial and patronizing. Nevertheless, in the best of the *Divine Songs,* Watts effectively and memorably employs poetry in the instruction of sometimes weighty theological truths, as in this quatrain on the work of Christ:

He honored all His Father's laws,
Which we have disobeyed;
He bore our sins upon the cross,
And our full ransom paid.[10]

In everything he wrote, Watts was in the business of employing his pen precisely to aid immature minds in grasping the transcendent truths of the gospel. Here, Watts laid out in four short lines the central doctrine of Christ's imputed righteousness, His active obedience, and His passive obedience, whereby he underwent the pain and suffering on the cross that we deserved for our guilt.

LULLABY

In his *Divine Songs*, Watts elevated the lullaby to charming theological depth with his "Hush! My Dear, Lie Still and Slumber."[11] At first blush, it appears to be another charming cradle song, sung from the point of view of a mother rocking and cooing gently to her child as the baby squirms and flails against sleep. It is a masterwork of the genre, but Watts takes it further. In fourteen stanzas, he richly develops an intimate comparison between an infant and the incarnate Son of God, and he lands where Watts always lands: he holds before the child redemption and free grace in Christ:

Hush! my dear, lie still and slumber,
Holy angels guard thy bed!
Heavenly blessings, without number,
Gently falling on thy head.

Sleep my babe; thy food and raiment,
House and home thy friends provide;
All without thy care or payment,
All thy wants are well supplied.

What happens next is a perfect representation of what Watts always does in his poetry. He takes the vivid scene he has created of a mother softly singing to her child and makes a beeline for Bethlehem, where Jesus "became a child like thee":

How much better thou'rt attended
Than the Son of God could be;
When from heaven he descended,
And became a child like thee!

Soft and easy is thy cradle,
Coarse and hard thy Savior lay;
When his birth-place was a stable,
And his softest bed was hay.

Blessed babe! what glorious features,
Spotless fair, divinely bright!
Must he dwell with brutal creatures!
How could angels bear the sight!

Was there nothing but a manger
Cursed sinners could afford,
To receive the heavenly stranger!
Did they thus affront their Lord!

Then Watts, as if the story and the "brutal creatures" might have upset the infant, creates a poetic interlude wherein the singer comes back to the present and, as a protective mother, promises to guard her baby:

Soft, my child; I did not chide thee,
Though my song might sound too hard,
'Tis thy mother sits beside thee,
And her arms shall be thy guard.

When he resumes the song, the maternal singer becomes "angry while I sing" at how the divine child was abused by His people:

Yet to read the shameful story,
How the Jews abused their King;
How they served the Lord of glory,
Makes me angry while I sing.

See the kinder shepherds round him,
Telling wonders from the sky!
Where they sought him, there they found him,
With his virgin mother by.

See the lovely babe a dressing;
Lovely infant, how he smiled!
When he wept, the mother's blessing
Soothed and hushed the holy child.

Lo, he slumbers in his manger,
Where the horned oxen fed;

Peace, my darling, here's no danger,
Here's no ox a-near thy bed.

Watts is never far from the gospel of grace, and here he
expands his imagination to include the punishment children
deserve for their sins and the cosmic rescue Jesus came to
accomplish as Redeemer and substitute for lost children:

'Twas to save thee, child, from dying,
Save my dear from burning flame,
Bitter groans and endless crying,
That thy blest Redeemer came.

May'st thou live to know and fear him,
Trust and love him all thy days;
Then go dwell for ever near him,
See his face, and sing his praise!

I could give thee thousand kisses,
Hoping what I most desire;
Not a mother's fondest wishes
Can to greater joys aspire!

It is difficult to imagine a man who never married,
who never fathered children, who never watched his wife
mothering his firstborn—a gawky bachelor such as Isaac
Watts—being capable of penning such a tender lullaby. But
while he never personally was a parent, he was a keen observer

of others in his life who were. Perhaps there is an implicit tribute in these fourteen stanzas to his own mother, Sarah Taunton Watts,[12] who may have been the inspiration for the persona offering a "thousand kisses," hoping in Christ for her children, her longing heart cooing the gospel to her son in words that, under the poetic devotion of that son, became this immortal cradle song.

"I SING THE ALMIGHTY POWER OF GOD"

The second song in *Divine Songs*, "I Sing the Almighty Power of God," is written in praise of God's providence in the world, and it has risen to become one of the finest of Watts' hymns— for children or adults. From the tiny flower to the "lofty skies," Watts, who loved the beauties of creation, explores the vastness of the earth God built by His almighty power. His thought progresses from first singing of the almighty power of God, to singing of God's wisdom, then to singing of His goodness "That filled the earth with food":

I sing th' almighty power of God
That made the mountains rise,
That spread the flowing seas abroad,
And built the lofty skies.
I sing the wisdom that ordained
The sun to rule the day;
The moon shines full at his command,
And all the stars obey.

I sing the goodness of the Lord
That filled the earth with food;
He formed the creatures with his word,
And then pronounced them good.
Lord, how thy wonders are displayed
Where'er I turn my eye,
If I survey the ground I tread
Or gaze upon the sky!

There's not a plant or flow'r below
But makes your glories known;
And clouds arise and tempests blow
By order from your throne;
While all that borrows life from you
Is ever in your care,
And everywhere that man can be,
You, God, are present there.[13]

The hymn originally included two more stanzas, but they have not survived the editors' knives through the centuries. Still, this hymn written for children underscores a central Watts theme of the sovereign rule of God over all his universe, and it underscores the wonder that so engulfed Watts at God's handiwork seen in that universe. His fourth stanza perfectly illustrates Watts' sense of awe at these things:

Lord, how your wonders are displayed
Where'er I turn my eye,

If I survey the ground I tread
Or gaze upon the sky.

Watts illustrated in his poetry what the Dutch statesman and pastor Abraham Kuyper famously put in prose: "There is not a square inch in the whole domain of our human existence over which Christ, who is Sovereign over all, does not cry: 'Mine!'"[14] Or, as the psalmist has it: "The heavens declare the glory of God, and the sky above proclaims his handiwork. Day to day pours out speech, and night to night reveals knowledge. There is no speech, nor are there words, whose voice is not heard. Their voice goes out through all the earth, and their words to the end of the world" (19:1–4). Likewise, as the Apostle Paul put it, "[God's] invisible attributes, namely, His eternal power and divine nature, have been clearly perceived, ever since the creation of the world, in the things that have been made. So they are without excuse" (Rom. 1:20).

If he had had only a poetic genius and not a doxological genius, Watts would have been an empty shell. The poet who scorned the "excess baggage of intricate form as well as of poetic adornment"[15] achieved Christ-honoring greatness with his enduring hymns because "His mind was saturated with the words of the Bible."[16]

WATTS: CHRIST-LIKE CARE FOR CHILDREN

Though given a mind of genius proportion, Watts cared deeply about the education and nurture of little children. Far from his brilliance making him indifferent to little ones, Watts marshaled all his skill winsomely to communicate gospel truth to their immature minds. But we do not always get this right; we are never far from twisting good things into "god" things and distorting truth. Nowhere is this more seen than when we Christians rediscover the importance of higher learning and then begin to aspire to cerebral greatness. From these lofty ambitions, it is only a short step to forgetting the way children learn and neglecting the way they understand truth. Watts never did this. With zeal and purposefulness, he set about to capture the minds and imaginations of the weakest and the youngest around him.

Though it may earn us the contempt of the sophisticated world, may we be those who invest our skills, our money, our time, and our gifts in children. We may be rebuked for doing so, as Jesus was by His disciples. C. S. Lewis was scorned by the intellectual elites at Oxford for writing for children, but he persisted, and Watts did the same.

So did the psalmists. There was no junior psalter in old covenant worship; they didn't need one, for the Holy Spirit intended the Psalms to be for everybody. So Watts set about versifying the Psalms in English so all people, big and small, educated and illiterate, might sing the praises of Jesus.

CHAPTER EIGHT

Watts as Psalm Interpreter

In his preface to *Divine Songs Attempted in Easy Language for the Use of Children*, Isaac Watts claimed to be cutting short his work of poems for children in order to get back to work on his poetic interpretation of the Psalms. He had been encouraged to imitate the Psalms by classmates when still a teen at Newington Academy, and his brother Enoch had often encouraged Watts to undertake the project. "There is a great need of a pen," Enoch wrote, "as vigorous and lively as yours, to quicken and revive the dying devotion of the age, to which nothing can afford such assistance as poetry contrived on purpose to elevate us even above ourselves."[1] Another letter, this one from his longtime friend John Hughes, written November 6, 1697, reveals that Watts began his work on the Psalms more than two decades before publishing *The Psalms of David*

Imitated in the Language of the New Testament, and Applied to the Christian State and Worship (1719). Hughes wrote, "I give you my hearty thanks for your ingenious paraphrase, in which you have so generously rescued the noble Psalmist out of the butcherly hands of Sternhold and Hopkins."[2]

It is critical to note that Watts' friend did not denigrate the inspired Psalms themselves. It was the "butchery" of the well-intentioned versifiers, Thomas Sternhold and John Hopkins, who were held by custom to a requirement of strict phrase-by-phrase metering of the English Psalms. Like Hughes, Watts also "protested against the dullness and crudity of expression, and the total lack of the New Testament Gospel in the contents of the Psalms," writes Erik Routley, again speaking not of the Psalms themselves but of their clumsy handling in English verse. As a poet, Watts particularly was "offended by the gawkiness of Barton's Psalms," yet another inadequate version used in his early years. Through all this, Watts began to ask himself: "Why may we no longer sing of Christ as God? When Christ makes all things new, why must our praises remain in the Old Covenant?"[3] Out of these musings, the idea for an entirely new method of interpreting and paraphrasing the Psalms in verse began forming in Watts' imagination.

THE REGULATIVE PRINCIPLE

The regulative principle of worship holds that nothing should be done in worship that is not specifically prescribed in Holy

Scripture. However, many in the Reformation tradition were divided as to whether this principle forbade the singing of non-inspired hymns. Since the Reformation, Lutherans had sung hymns of human composition along with Psalms in worship. Though John Calvin commended the singing of Psalms in French, he never specifically forbade hymns, and he may have written the psalm-like hymn "I Greet Thee, Who My Sure Redeemer Art" himself. Either way, he included it in the *Geneva Psalter* of 1551, a strong indication that he did not hold to exclusive psalmody.

Subsequent Calvinists, however, strained the regulative principle to the exclusion of any human poetry composed for singing in divine services. In Britain, exclusive psalmody ruled the day. Sadly, however, many of the well-meaning efforts at versifying the Psalm texts in English rhyme and meter fall far short of the splendors of the original Hebrew poetry.

DAVID THE CHRISTIAN

Watts made no apologies for his frontal assault on the prevailing Psalm versifications of Sternhold and Hopkins, as well as that of Nahum Tate and Nicholas Brady, who produced a collection of psalm versifications in 1696. There is no question that these were often awkward, and many of them were virtually unsingable. So Watts borrowed the redemptive-historical hermeneutic employed by the best preachers and developed from it a method of poetically interpreting and applying the

Psalms for singing in worship. His defense of his method indicates that Watts wanted the Old Testament to be understood in light of its fulfillment in Christ:

> Where the Psalmist . . . speaks of the pardon of sin through the mercies of God, I have added the merits of a Savior. Where he talks of sacrificing goats or bullocks, I rather choose to mention the sacrifice of Christ, the Lamb of God. Where he promises abundance of wealth, honor, and long life, I have changed some of these typical blessings for grace, glory, and life eternal, which are brought to light by the Gospel, and promised in the New Testament. And I am fully satisfied, that more honor is done to our blessed Savior by speaking his name, his graces, his actions, in his own language, according to the brighter discoveries he hath now made, than by going back again to the Jewish forms of worship, and the language of types and figures.[4]

It did not make sense to Watts that new covenant saints should refrain from taking the name of Jesus, "our blessed Savior," on their lips in their singing. He understood that Jewish forms of worship, the types and shadows of the gospel in the old covenant, were, as Paul put it, "being brought to an end" (2 Cor. 3:7), that "what once had glory has come to have no glory at all, because of the glory that surpasses it" (v. 10). Watts believed that by singing only the crude English Psalm versifications, a veil remained over the hearts of new covenant worshipers, and that "only through Christ is it taken away" (v. 14).

It is important to recall that Watts wrote his hymns and interpreted the Psalms in poetry alongside his duties as a preacher of the gospel. He knew that it was unconscionable of him as a preacher to neglect to show his flock Christ, who appears as the fulfillment of the law in all the Scriptures—and, hence, in the Psalms. For Watts, redemptive-historical poetic interpretation of the Psalms was the only hermeneutic, just as it was when he was preaching.

Watts was not actually being hermeneutically innovative here, as some suggest. All of his learning had been in the Reformed and Calvinist tradition, so he was merely attempting to urge a continuity between Christ-centered, Reformed preaching and Reformed singing in worship. Calvin himself had written: "We ought to read the Scriptures with the express design of finding Christ in them. Whoever shall turn aside from this object, though he may weary himself throughout his whole life in learning, will never attain the knowledge of the truth."[5] When he was called to be the preacher in John Owen's London pulpit, Watts had declared himself to the congregation to be "of the same mind with your former reverend pastor, Dr. John Owen,"[6] who had written of redemptive-historical preaching decades before Watts' Psalms were released, saying, *"Keep still Jesus Christ in your eye, in the perusal of the Scriptures, as the end, scope, and substance thereof; think Christ as the very substance, marrow, soul, and scope of the whole of Scriptures."*[7]

Later C. H. Spurgeon, who was bribed as a boy into memorizing many of Watts' hymns, wrote of how he interpreted Scripture: "I take whatever particular text I am in and I make a beeline for the Cross."[8]

The best expositors understand that Christ-centered interpretation is not a matter of methodological taste that works for some and not for others. J. I. Packer writes: "Christ is the true subject matter of Scripture: all was written to bear witness to him. He is the sum of the whole Bible, prophesied, typified, prefigured, exhibited, demonstrated, to be found in every leaf, almost in every line, the Scriptures being but as it were the swaddling bands of the child Jesus."[9] In his book *Christ-Centered Preaching*, Bryan Chapell writes, "The redemptive-historical method . . . is a vital and foundational tool that expositors need to accurately and gracefully interpret texts in their full context."[10] For Watts, no other method got at the burden of the psalm text before him—Jesus.

Some accuse Watts of tampering with divine inspiration by his handling of the Psalms. However, few had as high a view of the Psalms as Watts, and no doubt if he had grown up in the ancient Hebrew-speaking world where the inspired poetry and content remained pristine, undiminished by translation, Watts might have come up with another method. Erik Routley commented on what Watts was doing:

Let a man wonder and share his wonder with his fellows in the church—thus said Watts, and where did he get this but from the Psalms themselves? Where is there such cosmic vision, such pure and self-denying wonder as there? Watts protested against the lack of Christian Gospel in the Psalms, but he took from them that quality of wonder which made him, even at his least inspired moments, a man with the poet's touch.[11]

Observe how, in Watts' imitation of Psalm 136, like a good expositor in a sermon, he turns his hearer's face toward Christ:

He sent his Son with pow'r to save
From guilt and darkness and the grave:
Wonders of grace to God belong;
Repeat his mercies in your song.[12]

In this method of poetically and theologically interpreting the Psalms, Watts may have been further informed by Paul, who wrote that we are to do everything, "in word or deed," in the name of the Lord Jesus, and he wrote this in the immediate context of singing "psalms and hymns and spiritual songs" (Col 3:16–17). For Watts, what was true of preaching in new covenant worship was equally true of singing. His near-contemporary, Blaise Pascal, articulated the redemptive-historical hermeneutic of the Reformers and their offspring: "Without the Scripture, which have Jesus Christ alone as their object, we can know nothing."[13]

Armed with this understanding, Watts wanted David to sing the song of a Christian, and so he set to work.

"JESUS SHALL REIGN"

"The hymns of Luther," a Jesuit critic said, "killed more souls than his sermons."[14] Protestants would disagree, but Luther may be remembered more for his hymns than his sermons. The same is true of Watts. One reason is that he combined his redemptive-historical interpretation with vigorous poetry adorning the highest object. Perhaps one of the most concise examples of Watts' method is seen in his poetic interpretation of Psalm 72. The English prose version begins, "Give the king your justice, O God," and is clearly a psalm about King Solomon. But through Watts' redemptive-historical theology and his poetic skill, it became a Jesus-centered declaration of the gospel foreshadowed in the psalm and fulfilled in Christ:

> *Jesus shall reign where'er the sun*
> *Doth his successive journeys run;*
> *His kingdom stretch from shore to shore,*
> *Till moons shall wax and wane no more.*

> *To him shall endless prayer be made,*
> *And praises throng to crown his head;*
> *His name, like sweet perfume, shall rise*
> *With every morning sacrifice.*

Blessings abound where'er he reigns:
The pris'ner leaps to lose his chains,
The weary find eternal rest,
And all the sons of want are blest.

Let every creature rise and bring
Peculiar honors to our King;
Angels, descend with songs again,
And earth repeat the loud amen![15]

Once again, Watts dazzles the worshiper with wonder at the sovereign rule of Jesus over all His Kingdom. Set to the incomparable Scottish tune *Duke Street* by John Hatton (1793) forty-five years after Watts' death, this psalm-inspired hymn deserves to be a perennial favorite of every generation of Christians who long to "rise and bring peculiar honors to our King."

In the annals of the British Empire, a compelling story is told of Watts' Psalm 72. In 1762, King George III gathered in the South Sea Islands one thousand chiefs from Tonga, Fiji, and Samoa "to declare his islands Christian" and to further establish British rule. The proceedings began with an Anglican service in which "old chiefs and warriors who had shared the perils of many a battle" sang with their new emperor Watts' "Jesus Shall Reign."[16] I am fairly certain that Watts, the Nonconformist, would not have approved of the imperial comingling of church and state, but the anecdote illustrates how pervasively Watts had become synonymous, not only with sung Christian worship, but with the so-called Christian world.

Yet another memorable story is told that demonstrates the pervasive reach of Watts' poetry. In June 1925, after completing his theological training in Scotland, Eric Liddell boarded the train at Edinburgh's Waverly Station. A gold medalist in the 1924 Olympics, Liddell had become nothing short of a celebrity, and the station platform was crowded with a host of well-wishers, jostling to see him off. Leaving behind his beloved Scotland for mission work in China, Liddell was at a loss for words. What could he say to the vast crowd, eager to hear his final farewell? Ordinary words seemed insufficient. So Liddell broke into Watts' versification of Psalm 72, "Jesus Shall Reign." As the train jolted away from the platform, the entire crowd joined him in singing this immortal hymn— everyone singing by memory without hymnals.[17]

THE FINEST PSALMS

To be candid, not everything Watts wrote *in The Psalms of David Imitated in the Language of the New Testament* was an improvement on the "butchery" of the past. Just as a relatively small handful of his 750 hymns rose to the level of timeless and enduring classics, there is some "very poor stuff"[18] among his psalms, according to one hymnologist who otherwise praises Watts' skill.

Yet there are those who consider Watts' Psalm 90, "Our God, Our Help in Ages Past" (1719) to be his very finest hymn, even finer than "When I Survey." There is a grand scope and power to the poetry of the psalm, which opens with a focus on the entire sweep of human history and God's unalterable promise that He will be His people's help, their hope, and their "shelter from the stormy blast":

Our God, our help in ages past,
Our hope for years to come,
Our shelter from the stormy blast,
And our eternal home.[19]

In his second stanza, Watts' eyes may have scanned ahead to the language of Psalm 91:4, "He will cover you with his pinions, and under his wings you will find refuge":

Under the shadow of your throne
Your saints have dwelt secure;
Sufficient is your arm alone,
And our defense is sure.

Watts then returns to the second verse of Psalm 90 and roots his argument by transporting us back to creation, before "earth received her frame." He assures us that, though life has troubles and challenges, God is God, "to endless years the same":

Before the hills in order stood,
Or earth received her frame,
From everlasting you are God,
To endless years the same.

He then draws from verse 4 of Psalm 90, which illustrates that God is not confined by time as we know it; rather, He is infinitely above time: "a thousand years in your sight are but as yesterday when it is past, or as a watch in the night":

A thousand ages in your sight
Are like an evening gone;
Short as the watch that ends the night
Before the rising sun.

But the "busy tribes of flesh and blood" are not like the infinite God, eternal and unchangeable as He is. We human beings "are carried downward by the flood" of time and decay; we die and are forgotten:

The busy tribes of flesh and blood,
With all their lives and cares,
Are carried downwards by the flood,
And lost in following years.

Watts had a particular genius for putting things in their proper perspective. Here, he has contrasted the eternality and